Richard
WRIGHT

Richard WRIGHT

A BIOGRAPHY

DEBBIE LEVY

Twenty-First Century Books
Minneapolis

Twenty-First Century Books
A division of Lerner Publishing Group, Inc.
241 First Avenue North
Minneapolis, MN 55401 U.S.A.

Website address: www.lernerbooks.com

Library of Congress Cataloging-in-Publication Data

Levy, Debbie.
Richard Wright / by Debbie Levy.
p.   cm. —   (Literary greats)
Includes bibliographical references and index.
ISBN: 978–0–8225–6793–6 (lib. bdg. : alk. paper)
1. Wright, Richard, 1908–1960—Juvenile literature. 2. Authors, American—
20th century—Biography—Juvenile literature. 3. African American authors—
Biography—Juvenile literature. I. Title.

PS3545.R815Z675 2008   813'.52—dc22 [B]   2006101189

Manufactured in the United States of America
1 2 3 4 5 6 – BP – 13 12 11 10 09 08

The author gratefully acknowledges:

Ms. Julia Wright, for permission to quote from
White Man, Listen!, by Richard Wright (New York:
HarperPerennial, 1995) and from Richard Wright Reader
(New York: Da Capo Press, 1997).

John Hawkins & Associates, Inc., and Julia Wright for
permission to quote from the Richard Wright Papers in
the Yale Collection of American Literature.

Arcade Publishing, for permission to
reprint an excerpt from *Haiku: This Other World*, by
Richard Wright (New York: Arcade Publishing, 1998),
copyright © 1998 by Ellen Wright.

Contents

Introduction

Two friends walk into a coffee shop. The setting is Greenwich Village, a New York City neighborhood known as a tolerant community of artists, writers, and intellectuals. The time is 1947, two years after the end of World War II (1939–1945). New Yorkers are enjoying the benefits of peacetime, particularly the goods that were in short supply during the war, such as coffee.

The man and woman order their coffee. When the waitress serves them, they lift the cups to their lips, take a sip—and almost spit it out. The coffee is spiked with salt.

When they complain, the waitress is ready with an answer. "That's how we serve it here," she says to the man. "If you don't like it here, then go somewheres else."

Of course, the coffee shop did not normally serve salted coffee. Employees gave the unpalatable beverage only to African American customers, and the man in the coffee shop that day was African American—or Negro, the term he and others used at the time. In many restaurants in the United States, white owners and employees showed their hostility toward black patrons by putting salt in their coffee.

The man, Richard Wright, was the most famous black author in the United States. He had written two best-selling books, *Native Son* and *Black Boy*. Black and white readers alike bought

9

hundreds of thousands of copies of his books. Wright earned plenty of money from his literary success, enough to buy a large house on Charles Street in Greenwich Village. He was often an honored guest at literary events, and he appeared in the pages of newspapers and magazines across the country. Eleanor Roosevelt, wife of deceased U.S. president Franklin Delano Roosevelt, admired Wright's works.

But when it came to everyday life, none of these accomplishments mattered. On the streets of Greenwich Village, Wright noticed the hateful glares of some of his white neighbors. White shopkeepers called him "boy," even though he was a thirty-nine-year-old man. No local white barber would accept him as a customer. Wright had to go one hundred blocks north, to Harlem, an African American neighborhood, to get a haircut from a black barber.

The insults were nothing new to Wright. He had grown up around race hatred. He made it his mission as a writer to fight racism with words. But his writings did not sway the shopkeepers, neighbors, and waitresses who saw his skin color and treated him as inferior. And his words were powerless against the department store clerk who refused to let his five-year-old daughter, Julia, use the store's restroom.

Wright could not bear the thought of anybody treating his daughter as a second-class citizen. From an earlier trip to France, he saw that the French and other Europeans were color-blind compared to Americans. So, at the end of July 1947, the author of *Native Son* left his native land behind, in search of a place where skin color did not matter. Wright and his family moved to Paris, France. There he found the racial tolerance he craved. But no matter where he made his home, in Richard Wright's works and in his life, skin color would always matter.

1
Mississippi Beginnings

RICHARD NATHANIEL WRIGHT was born in an unwelcoming time and place for African Americans. The time was September 4, 1908, forty-five years after the end of slavery in the United States. Richard's grandparents had been slaves. In 1908 black people were free, but theirs was a limited freedom. Although white people no longer owned black people as slaves, whites kept blacks out of public schools, good jobs, nice neighborhoods—out of anything and anyplace the white people wanted for themselves.

The place was Adams County, Mississippi. Leading white citizens lived in stately mansions built before the Civil War (1861–1865). Black citizens were forced to live apart from whites, in separate neighborhoods. And Jim Crow lived everywhere. *Jim Crow* referred to the racist system of laws and customs that white Southerners had created to deprive African Americans of their basic rights.

Richard's father, Nathan Wright, could neither read nor write. He was a sharecropper—a farmer who owned no land of his own

For the first few years of his life, Richard lived in a sharecropper's shack like this one.

but farmed a white person's land. Richard's mother, Ella Wilson, had a modest education and had worked as a teacher for black children. But after she and Nathan Wright got married, Ella gave up teaching. The couple lived on a farm east of Natchez, Mississippi. Their home was a flimsy wooden shack.

FROM FARM TO TOWN

Ella and Nathan worked hard. But sharecropping was full of pitfalls. Sharecroppers had to get loans from merchants to buy seed and tools. In exchange for the loans, the sharecroppers pledged portions of their harvest to the merchants. They also turned over part of their harvest to the landowners, as rent for living on the farm. As a result many sharecroppers struggled constantly with debt.

Ella and Nathan could not beat a system that was stacked so heavily against them. In the fall of 1910, they had another baby boy, Leon. By the next year, they had given up the farm. Ella, Richard, and Leon moved in with Ella's parents, the Wilsons, in Natchez. Nathan worked as a traveling laborer before finding steadier work at a Natchez sawmill. Then he moved in with the Wilsons as well.

Natchez was a small port city on the Mississippi River. The population, half black and half white, was strictly segregated, or separated by race. The Wilsons were not wealthy, but their house in the town's black section was far more comfortable than Ella and Nathan's shack. The countryside around the town offered views of fields and woods.

Richard was a curious, observant boy. He later wrote of his delight in seeing "long straight rows of red and green vegetables stretching away in the sun to the bright horizon." He also remembered the earthiness of rural life: "There was the experience of feeling death without dying that came from watching a chicken leap about blindly after its neck had been snapped by a quick twist of my father's wrist."

Although the black citizens of Natchez suffered the pains and humiliations of Jim Crow, Richard did not yet grasp any distinction between black people and white people. In his own family, skin color varied across a wide range. His father, Nathan, was dark. His mother, Ella, was much lighter. And then there was Grandmother Wilson, Ella's mother. She was considered black under Southern law because she had some African ancestry. But her skin was white. She had Irish and Scottish ancestors, and with her smooth dark hair and sharp, narrow features, she looked much like the white people who lived in another section of town. For Richard, the notion of two different races seemed strange.

MEMPHIS STRUGGLES

In 1913, when Richard was four years old, Nathan and Ella decided to leave Natchez. They bought tickets on a paddle-wheel boat and traveled to Memphis, Tennessee, a city of nearly 100,000 people. Nathan hoped he would find a better job there.

Like Natchez, Memphis was strictly segregated. The Wrights rented two rooms in the black section of the city. Unlike the Wrights' home in Natchez, however, their Memphis neighborhood offered no pleasant views of fields or woods. It was grimy and urban, with few places for Richard and Leon to play.

Nathan Wright struggled to earn enough money to provide for his family. He found work as a night maintenance man at a drugstore. At home during the day, he expected his children to be quiet so he could sleep. This created tension between Richard and his father. Richard began to resent his father, whom he viewed as unkind and distant.

More and more often, Nathan went out to relax in the nightclubs on Beale Street, Memphis's main strip where African Americans could enjoy music and other entertainment. He brought home less money for Ella to buy food. Sometime in 1914, he stopped coming home at all.

"WHY COULD I NOT EAT?"

The responsibility of providing for Richard and Leon now fell to Ella. She hired herself out as a domestic servant for white families, helping cook and serve their meals. These jobs did not pay much, and the family often went hungry. Hunger became Richard's central concern. It made him even angrier at his father.

Sometimes Ella took the boys to work with her. Richard stood in the kitchen where his mother prepared delicious food for her white employers and waited to see if there would be any leftovers.

"Watching the white people eat would make my empty stomach churn and I would grow vaguely angry," he later wrote. "Why could I not eat when I was hungry? Why did I always have to wait until others were through?"

Most days when Ella went to work, she left behind a loaf of bread and a pot of tea for the boys. Neighbors kept an eye on Richard and Leon, but the two were mostly on their own. They found amusements in the streets, along with other children whose parents were at work. Some of their games were harmless pranks, such as tying a dead snake on a string and flinging it in front of unsuspecting passersby.

Ella Wright worked hard to care for her two sons. This photo of her was taken later in her life.

This photograph from a 1945 photo essay in Life *magazine recreates Richard's early days in Memphis based on his autobiography,* Black Boy, *which came out that year. Richard and his brother spent many days on their own while their mother was working.*

Other activities were not so harmless. Richard hung around a nearby saloon. He later wrote, "I was a drunkard in my sixth year, before I had begun school." This may have been an exaggeration, but his activities worried Ella enough that she found an older woman to watch her sons while she was at work.

Though he spent hours roaming the streets, Richard still had time to look through the books brought home by neighborhood schoolchildren. He decided he wanted to learn to decipher the marks on the pages. Ella helped him, and before long Richard was reading books and newspapers.

In 1915, at the age of seven, Richard began attending the Howe Institute, a school for black children. He learned easily, but at first he was so shy in the classroom that he became speechless when the teacher called on him.

Hunger was still a constant in Richard's life. One Sunday his mother invited the preacher from her church and a few neighbors to the apartment for a fried chicken dinner. Richard was thrilled at the prospect of such a fine meal. The first course was soup. The others ate their soup and turned to the platter of chicken in the center of the table. Anxious that there would be no chicken left for him, Richard found himself unable to swallow his soup. But Ella insisted that he eat his soup before getting any chicken. The preacher enjoyed one helping of chicken and then another. The platter's contents diminished. "That preacher's going to eat all the chicken!" Richard screamed. The preacher laughed.

Ella sent Richard away without dinner that day. Richard continued to like fried chicken—but he never did like church.

A WORLD TURNED UPSIDE DOWN

A few months after Richard started school, Ella became very sick. She felt weak and suffered pain, but no one could figure out exactly what was wrong. Grandmother Wilson came to help for a while, but she could not stay in Memphis. Her own husband had arthritis, and she needed to go home to care for him.

With Nathan Wright out of the family's life, Ella had few options. She could not look after her boys or work when she was so ill. Neighbors pitched in, but she needed a more reliable solution. In early 1916 Ella placed Richard and Leon in an orphanage for black children.

Richard hated the orphanage. It was a two-story structure in the middle of a grassy field. Instead of hiring someone to mow the lawn, the director made the children yank out overgrown grass around the building. Richard's world turned upside down as he found himself in a place without parents, without friends, and without a neighborhood.

After a few weeks, Richard ran away. A police officer discovered him walking through the streets and took him back to the orphanage. The director punished him with a spanking. Ella felt bad for her son. She took Richard to beg Nathan for money, but Nathan claimed to have none to spare. So Ella turned to one of her seven siblings. She and the boys would move to Elaine, Arkansas, where her favorite younger sister, Maggie, lived. Maggie and her husband invited Ella, Richard, and Leon to move in with them. It was the best offer the family had.

SUMMER AWAKENINGS

Before going to Arkansas, Ella and the boys stayed with her parents for several months. The Wilsons had moved from Natchez to Jackson, the capital of Mississippi. They were not as well off as they used to be. Richard Wilson's ailments kept him from working, and Margaret Wilson, a trained midwife, also worked less as she grew older. Still, they lived in a house with a garden.

Although the Wilsons lived on a city street, Richard and Leon could walk to nearby woods, a swamp, and the Pearl River. Richard enjoyed fishing with his grandfather and brother. He had fun playing outdoors with local children. And he appreciated one other thing in particular: "There was the drugged, sleepy feeling that came from sipping glasses of milk," he later wrote, "drinking them slowly so that they would last a long time, and drinking enough for the first time in my life."

While spending the summer of 1916 in Jackson, Richard discovered the world of fiction. To help make ends meet, the Wilsons rented a room in their house to a young teacher named Eloise Crawford. Richard saw her reading novels and asked her to tell him the stories.

Crawford hesitated to share her books with Richard. She knew—as did Richard—that Grandmother Wilson strongly disapproved of novels. Granny followed a very strict form of the Seventh-day Adventist religion, a Christian denomination. She believed that lying was a sin and that fiction was a form of lying because it was not true.

Richard persisted, and Crawford finally agreed to tell him one of the stories she was reading—the story of Bluebeard. In this suspenseful, bloody fairy tale, a curious young woman becomes the

A 1945 Life *magazine article included this recreation of Richard's days living in his grandparents' house in Mississippi.*

Living in Jackson, Mississippi, in 1916, Richard discovered the world of fiction. He also learned about racial discrimination.

eighth wife of Bluebeard, a rich but mysterious nobleman. Bluebeard is known for two things: his frightening appearance and the disappearances of his first seven wives. Crawford started to whisper the story to Richard. He later described his reaction: "The tale made the world around me be, throb, live. . . . My sense of life deepened and the feel of things was different, somehow. . . . The sensations the story aroused in me were never to leave me."

Crawford did not get to tell Richard how the story ended, however, because his grandmother discovered them on the porch. She scolded them both furiously. They were both going to burn in hell, she told them.

Richard did not care. He was overtaken by the power of words. "I had tasted what to me was life, and I would have more of it, somehow, some way," he wrote.

Besides fairy tales, Richard was introduced to something less enchanting during his summer in Jackson. For the first time, he learned about the huge gap between black and white people in the South. He observed that white people enjoyed privileges that black people were denied. White people lived in their own parts of town, which were nicer than the black sections. White people could dine in any restaurant they wanted, while black people could eat only in black cafés. White people rode in comfortable train cars, while black people had to travel in the no-frills cars at the rear of the train.

Richard also heard from his black neighbors that white people disliked black people so much that whites sometimes beat and even killed blacks. He did not know of specific cases. He knew only that the world around him was more complicated, unfriendly, and dangerous than he had ever imagined.

2

Growing Up With Jim Crow

IN THE LATE SUMMER OF 1916, Richard and his family moved, as planned, to Arkansas to live with Aunt Maggie and her husband, Silas Hoskins. Uncle Silas owned a successful saloon in the town of Elaine. He and Maggie welcomed Ella, Richard, and Leon into their home, a comfortable bungalow. Richard enjoyed his aunt's company, especially after the strict atmosphere of Granny's house. He also enjoyed the abundance of food.

"Can I eat all I want?" he asked when he first sat down to supper and saw platters of food piled high.

"Eat as much as you like," Uncle Silas said. Richard's uncle did not have to tell him twice.

Life in Elaine was sweet for Richard. He had plenty to eat. He had places to play. But the race hatred Richard was learning about soon struck home. Uncle Silas's successful business made some white citizens jealous. They threatened to kill him. One day, just a few months after Richard and his family had moved to Elaine,

Uncle Silas did not return home from his saloon. Dinnertime came and went, and still he did not show up. Then a neighbor brought the terrible news: a white man had shot Uncle Silas to death.

Screaming, Aunt Maggie started running down the road toward the saloon. But the neighbor reported that the whites in town said they would kill Silas's family next. Ella forced her sister back into the house. A few hours later, the two women and the two children ran away from their home, their belongings packed hastily in a wagon. They fled to West Helena, a nearby town. Aunt Maggie could not even retrieve Uncle Silas's body, so they could not give him a funeral.

POVERTY AND PAIN

In West Helena, the family moved into the poor black section of town. Ella and Maggie supported themselves by working in white people's homes. While the women were at work, Richard and Leon took to the streets. Ella left the boys ten cents for lunch, which they spent on gingersnaps and Coca-Cola. Richard absorbed the fear and anger that the other neighborhood children felt toward whites—hatred in return for hatred. And he heard from the other children that many black people wanted to move to the North. There, they said, white people did not hate black people as much as Southern whites did, and blacks could get better jobs.

Aunt Maggie did move North, to Detroit, Michigan. Ella and the boys remained in West Helena. In the fall of 1918, Richard and Leon started attending the neighborhood school for black children. At ten years old, Richard had had hardly any schooling. Still, he was able to read and write, and he was a fast learner. But Ella fell sick suddenly, with the same unknown illness she had experienced in Memphis. Once again, Richard had to leave school, this time to earn money. He did odd jobs, such as delivering lunch to workers in the railway yard and carrying firewood and laundry to people's homes.

Ella's health worsened. One day Richard found her in bed. She was paralyzed, unable to move the left side of her body. Neighbors helped care for her and the boys and sent word to Grandmother Wilson about what had happened. A doctor determined that Ella had suffered a stroke. Although Richard disliked his grandmother's strict and dour ways, he found himself desperately hoping that she would come and help him.

HUNGER AGAIN

Granny traveled to West Helena and brought Ella, Richard, and Leon back with her to Jackson. Ella's brothers and sisters gathered at the house to help sort out matters. The adults decided that Leon would go to Detroit with Aunt Maggie. Richard would live with his uncle Clark in Greenwood, Mississippi, not far from Jackson.

Although Uncle Clark and his wife, Aunt Jody, had a nice house and plenty of food, Richard could not get comfortable there. He started school in Greenwood but found it hard to concentrate. He begged to go back to his mother. Finally Uncle Clark bought him a ticket and put him on a train to Jackson.

At the Wilsons' home, Richard had his mother but not much else. He suffered from hunger again. Between the Wilsons' poverty and Granny's religious dietary restrictions, there was not much to eat. Pork, a mainstay of the Southern diet, was forbidden. For breakfast the family ate cornmeal mush. Supper was likely to be greens. Richard wanted to earn money so that he could buy better food. Many children in the neighborhood had jobs on Saturday. But Grandmother Wilson would not let Richard work on that day, which was the Sabbath, or holy day of rest, in the Adventist faith.

Grandmother Wilson was a very sober woman. She and Richard often did not see eye-to-eye on things.

"Once again I knew hunger, biting hunger," Richard wrote later. "No food that I could dream of seemed half so utterly delicious as vanilla wafers. Every time I had a nickel I would run to the corner grocery store and buy a box of vanilla wafers and walk back home, slowly, so that I could eat them all up without having to share with anyone. Then I would sit on the front steps and dream of eating another box."

TROUBLE IN THE FAMILY

Richard was not the only young person in the Wilson household. The youngest Wilson daughter, Addie, had just finished high school.

She was only nine years older than Richard, but she was his aunt. Addie, like her mother, was a Seventh-day Adventist. She lived with her parents and taught at the nearby Adventist church school.

In September 1920, Richard turned twelve and returned to school. He wanted to go to the public school for black children, the Jim Hill School, but Grandmother Wilson wanted him in the Adventist school. Richard's aunt Addie was the only teacher at the school, so he sat in her classroom along with thirty other students of all ages.

Richard was already chafing against the strict religion and discipline at home. At school, too, he faced correction and authority from his young aunt. One day Addie found walnut shells on the floor near Richard's seat. She gave him a rap on the knuckles for eating in class. When Richard started to explain, she ordered him to the front of the classroom, where she struck his hand repeatedly with a switch. It hurt, but he did not cry. He was not going to let his aunt think that he cared.

At home after school, Aunt Addie came at Richard again with a switch. Not only had he eaten walnuts in class, she complained, but he was also disrespectful to her. Something in Richard snapped. He had had enough. With his aunt pursuing him, he grabbed a knife from the kitchen and turned on her. When he refused to drop it, they ended up wrestling on the floor. Grandmother Wilson and Ella, still limping from her stroke, heard the commotion and broke up the fight.

Richard had not eaten the walnuts in class. Another boy had. But that did not matter to his family. To his grandparents and aunt, he was trouble. To his mother, he was a constant source of worry.

HUNGRY FOR STORIES

One good thing came out of Richard's rebellion. He was allowed to enroll in the Jim Hill Public School in the fall of 1921. As far

At the Jim Hill Public School in Jackson, Mississippi, Richard advanced from fifth to sixth grade in just a few weeks.

as Grandmother Wilson was concerned, he was a lost cause to her faith. He might as well go to a nonreligious school.

Although he was thirteen, Richard was placed in the fifth grade—two years behind his age group—because he had had so little schooling. In just a few weeks, however, his teacher promoted him to sixth grade. Richard was proud of himself. He mastered his lessons quickly. Since he could finish his schoolwork before the other children, he started bringing magazines to class to read.

Richard also liked becoming part of the group of kids at school. But he felt differences between himself and the others. At lunchtime, when the other children bought sandwiches at the neighborhood store, he could not. He was too proud to admit he did not have enough money. As his classmates bit into their sardine sandwiches and asked him why he didn't have lunch, he said, "Aw, I'm not hungry at noon, ever."

Of course Richard was hungry for lunch. He was also hungry for something else. He had a voracious appetite for stories, especially crime and horror and fantasy stories. Reading led to writing. As he later explained, "Some people go to the sea shore and see people swimming and they want to swim too. When I started to read I wanted to write." And so he started writing stories.

"YOU'LL NEVER BE A WRITER"

Richard finally got the chance to work during the summer after sixth grade, in 1922. A neighbor, Mr. Mance, sold burial insurance to poor black farmers across Mississippi. The insurance would pay for their casket and burial when they died. He asked Richard to travel with him to help customers fill out insurance forms.

Driving with Mr. Mance from one sharecropper's shack to another, Richard saw a side of black life that depressed him. The farmers and their children could not read or write. While Richard appreciated the endless glasses of milk his hosts gave him, he felt bad that they were poor and illiterate. "I saw a bare, bleak pool of black life," he wrote later, "and I hated it."

But he did like the money he earned. When he started back to school in the fall of 1922, he badgered his grandmother about getting a job that included Saturday hours. After he threatened to run away, she relented.

Nearly all jobs for young black teens involved working for white people. And this, Richard learned, involved paying respect, even when employers treated him poorly, and holding his tongue, even when he was longing to speak. When Richard applied for his first job with a white family, the woman who interviewed him asked him whether he was a thief. Without thinking, Richard laughed. The woman asked for an explanation. Richard pointed out that if he were a thief, he would not tell her. When he saw her getting angry, he hung his head and said quietly that he did not steal. She hired him.

Richard did not mind the duties—chopping wood, bringing in coal for the stove, washing, sweeping, and waiting on the family at breakfast. But on his first day, his employer expressed surprise that a black boy would remain in school for seventh grade. When Richard explained that he wanted to continue his schooling so that he could be a writer—one of the first times he said that out loud—she responded, "You'll never be a writer. Who on earth put such ideas into your nigger head?" Richard did not return to work the next day.

He got other jobs. With the money he earned, he bought clothes and lunch at school. He bought schoolbooks, as well as the cheap novels and crime magazines he loved. He now knew, like so many other black people, that working in the white world was frequently humiliating and unfair. But at least Richard and his friends from school could compare notes and joke about it.

DREAMS OF ESCAPE

As Richard began seventh grade, his mother's health improved. She and Richard talked about getting their own home again. But events clouded their dreams. Grandfather Wilson died in November 1922. Soon afterward, Ella suffered more paralysis from another stroke.

The next fall, in 1923, Richard got a job with the first friendly white family he had ever met. He was in eighth grade at Smith Robertson School. Still an excellent student, Richard dreamed more and more of writing stories and publishing them in magazines and books. Soon he went beyond dreaming: in the spring of 1924, Richard wrote his first complete short story.

Smith Robertson was the first public school in Jackson, Mississippi, to be built for African Americans.

Little is known for certain about this story, because no copy has survived. Richard later said he called it "The Voodoo of Hell's Half-Acre" and that it was about a villain who plotted to steal a widow's home. He took it to the *Southern Register*, a weekly newspaper by and about the black citizens of Jackson. The editor agreed to publish the story in installments over three weeks. He could not offer payment, but he was one of the only adults in Richard's life who encouraged his interest in writing.

Richard's first experience as a published author brought him attention—almost none of it positive. His grandmother called fiction the devil's work. Aunt Addie pointed out that using the word *hell* in the title was a sin. Richard's mother worried that his writing stories would make people think he was "weak-minded."

None of these reactions made Richard doubt his desire to become a writer. Instead, he felt angry with the people around him. He imagined moving to a place where he could follow his dream of writing books, where people would consider his writing a good thing. He dreamed of going to the North.

Events during the summer of 1924 reinforced Richard's feeling that he needed to leave the South. Local white men murdered a classmate's brother when they learned that he was romantically involved with a white woman. At first the young man was reported shot to death—but he was not so lucky. Instead, the white mob subjected him to a lynching and tortured him to death.

The lynching depressed and frightened Richard. The rules for black people in the South were harsh and unforgiving. "The penalty of death awaited me if I made a false move," Richard wrote, "and I wondered if it was worth-while to make any move at all."

IN HIS OWN WORDS

In the spring of 1925, Richard and other ninth graders at Smith Robertson School prepared for graduation. The principal, W. H. Lanier, selected sixteen-year-old Richard and four other top students to speak at the ceremony. Richard wrote a speech addressing the ways in which the Jim Crow educational system robbed black people of the chance to become complete human beings.

Before graduation Lanier brought Richard into his office and handed him some papers. This was the speech—written by Lanier—that Richard was to read at graduation. Lanier made it clear that Richard would not give a speech criticizing white people. After much effort, the principal had just persuaded Jackson's white leaders to allow him to open the first public high school in Jackson for black children. Lanier did not want to jeopardize the new school.

Richard (back row, fifth from right) *stands with his ninth-grade graduating class at Smith Robertson in 1925. Richard, always a good student, excelled at Smith Robertson and ended up graduating at the top of his class.*

Richard would have none of it. He would deliver his speech or no speech at all. Hearing of the conflict, his family and friends urged him to do as the principal asked. Richard was adamant, and Lanier relented. If Richard toned down his more strident passages, he could give his own speech. Richard was willing to compromise that much. On May 29, 1925, dressed in his first suit with long pants, he delivered "The Attributes of Life." He spoke from memory. When he finished speaking, he walked out of the room and away from his classmates and teachers and went home.

THE WAY OUT

Richard's goal was to leave Mississippi and eventually make his way to Chicago, Illinois. As a first step, he planned to go to Memphis. First he had to save enough money to buy a train ticket and to support himself as he was settling down in a new place.

While some of his friends went on to tenth grade in the fall of 1925 at the new black high school—Lanier High School, named for Principal Lanier—Richard went to work. He got a job at a clothing store but was soon fired because he did not behave the way his bosses thought black people should: cheerful and servile. He ran into trouble at other jobs for similar reasons. A black friend from school tried to coach Richard on how to act around white people. He should get out of their way. He should not speak his mind. He should definitely not act smart. Learning to act the fool was much harder for Richard than learning his school lessons.

Richard grew impatient. It would take many months of work to save the one hundred dollars he wanted in his pocket before leaving Jackson. With hesitation, but also with determination, he decided to raise the money illegally. A classmate told him about a movie theater run by a white man where some black employees had a scheme to steal money from ticket sales. The owner was looking for a new ticket collector, and the employees were hoping for someone to join their scheme. Richard got the job. He helped cheat the owner out of his cash. In two weeks, Richard had his one hundred dollars.

To pad his pockets a little more, Richard stole canned food from nearby Jackson College and a gun from a neighbor. He sold those items and bought a cheap cardboard suitcase, some clothes, and shoes. On a cold, rainy Saturday night in November 1925, he bid his mother good-bye. He promised to send for her and Leon. Then Richard walked to the railroad station and boarded a train to Memphis. He rode, as required by Jim Crow, in the all-black car.

3
Heading North

IN THE DECADE since the Wrights had lived in Memphis, the city had grown. Black people made up more than one-third of its population of 160,000. Although racism was alive and well in Memphis, African Americans enjoyed a vibrant culture and community. The Beale Street nightclubs were thriving. Memphis was the capital of the new style of music known as the blues. A black bandleader named William Christopher (W. C.) Handy introduced this plaintive music.

New in town, Wright immediately got a job as a dishwasher at the same drugstore where his father had once worked. He found a cheap place to stay. Soon he found a better job at an optical company, running errands and washing eyeglass lenses, which were smeared and dirty after being processed in the optical machinery. Wright earned extra money doing deliveries and other small tasks for the white employees. They called him "boy" and used racial slurs in their matter-of-fact way, but Wright had learned to mask his anger at the daily humiliations of the Jim

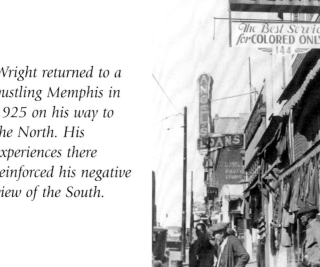

Wright returned to a bustling Memphis in 1925 on his way to the North. His experiences there reinforced his negative view of the South.

Crow South. He ate his lunch—usually a hamburger and a bag of peanuts—with other black men who worked in the same office building. Talk often turned to the way white people treated them. "Each of us hated and feared the whites," Wright later noted, "yet had a white man put in a sudden appearance we would have assumed silent, obedient smiles."

WORDS AS WEAPONS

Although Wright lived simply to save his money to move North, he allowed himself the luxury of buying reading material. His

reading tastes were changing from crime stories and sensational tales to literary magazines such as *Harper's* and the *Atlantic Monthly*. When he came across words he did not know, he looked them up in a pocket dictionary he carried with him.

In the spring of 1927, when Wright was eighteen, he read an article in the paper that changed his reading habits even more—and, in a way, even changed his life. The article was an editorial, or opinion piece, attacking a man Wright had never heard of before: H. L. Mencken. Mencken was an author who also edited

H. L. Mencken taught Wright that words could be used as a weapon. This photograph of Mencken was taken in the late 1920s.

a magazine called the *American Mercury*. From the tone of the editorial, Wright could tell that Mencken, a Northern white man, had progressive ideas about black people's rights. Wright had to see what Mencken had written that had so infuriated the white Southerner who wrote the piece.

Wright faced one problem: black people were not allowed to use the public library in Memphis. Undaunted, he approached one of his white coworkers for assistance. Wright's plan was to pretend he was at the library to pick up books for the white man. This had the ring of truth, as Wright had gone to the library in the past on such an errand. But this time he would bring a note signed by the coworker asking the librarian to give Wright the books. He would present the coworker's library card and, if things went as planned, get the books—for himself.

The white coworker went along with Wright's idea. That day, Wright composed the note. "Dear Madam," he wrote, "Will you please let this nigger boy have some books by H. L. Mencken?" Wright believed that using the common racial slur gave the note an authentic touch. And he asked the librarian to select the Mencken books simply because he did not know the titles of any of them.

The plan worked. The librarian selected two volumes by H. L. Mencken and handed them to Wright.

That night he dug into the books. His eyes opened to a world where people—some people, at least—were not afraid to say and write unpopular ideas that were sure to offend others. Mencken sharply criticized much about American culture. He ridiculed politicians, people who went to church, Southerners, writers he did not like—anything and anyone.

"I stood up," Wright recalled, "trying to realize what reality lay behind the meaning of the words. . . . Yes, this man was fighting, fighting with words. He was using words as weapons, using them as one would use a club. Could words be weapons? Well, yes, for here they were. Then, maybe, perhaps, I could use them as a weapon? No. It frightened me." But in addition to the fear, Wright felt excited and awakened.

CHICAGO BOUND

Wright kept reading and awakening. He read Sinclair Lewis, Theodore Dreiser, Sherwood Anderson, Stendhal, and Ivan Turgenev. Their novels realistically depicted society's flaws. Wright's sophistication grew, but he was careful to seem like an unschooled black man. He kept up his scheme at the library. "When a book I wanted wasn't in, I would never ask for another," he later told an interviewer. "Oh, no! I would go out, change the list, and come back again." He knew he was crossing a line between the white and black worlds.

As he expanded his horizons, Wright still lived in the limited world of the Jim Crow South. He supported himself with his menial job at the optical company. He scrimped on meals. Other

This photograph of downtown Chicago, Illinois, was taken around the time Wright moved there in 1927.

than his hamburger lunch, he ate bread and milk for breakfast and a can of pork and beans for dinner most days. He lived in a modest rented room. His scrimping paid off. By the fall of 1927, Wright had saved enough money to bring his mother and brother to Memphis. They were all that much closer to moving to Chicago.

Soon afterward, Aunt Maggie came back from Detroit to join the family. She was optimistic about job opportunities up North, and her enthusiasm was infectious. The family decided that Richard and Maggie would go first. In Chicago they would get jobs, save money, and send for Ella and Leon as soon as they could afford to.

In late 1927, Wright and his aunt boarded a train for Chicago, the second-largest city in the United States at the time. Aunt Maggie dreamed of opening her own beauty parlor. Wright had dreams, too. They were not just about getting a job or being able to afford a comfortable apartment and nourishing food. At age nineteen, he dreamed of a new life, one in which he could be comfortable in his own skin and his surroundings would nourish his mind and soul.

LAND OF KITCHENETTES

Wright and his aunt moved into a boardinghouse in Chicago's South Side. The South Side was an expanse of run-down apartment buildings chopped up into "kitchenettes"—tiny dwellings where black families lived in one room with a small kitchen area. White people had moved out of the neighborhood in the early 1900s, when African Americans from the South started heading north to Chicago. (This mass exodus from the South to the urban North lasted for more than half a century and became known as the Great Migration.) Chicago's South Side had become a ghetto of 200,000 black residents. The white owners of South Side buildings and businesses were happy to collect rent and sell liquor to black residents, but they were not interested in spending money to improve the neighborhood.

The morning after his arrival, Wright ventured into the cold Chicago winter in search of work. He took the streetcar to a white area, where he was more likely to find a job. On the streetcar, black people sat next to white people, which was unheard of in the South. In the storefronts, there were no "Whites Only" signs. Wright stopped at one of the stores, a delicatessen owned by a Jewish family, the Hoffmans, who had recently emigrated from Europe. They offered him a job. His duties were to make deliveries, clean the store, and keep the shelves filled with food.

The Hoffmans were friendly, and the deli was a decent place to work. But Wright felt uncomfortable. Unlike him, the Hoffmans could barely speak English. Unlike him, they were foreigners. Yet they owned a store and lived in a nicer part of town. They could do these things because they were white, and he could not because he was black. Wright realized that even though he had left behind the overt Jim Crow racism of the South, he still faced race discrimination. As he took the streetcar each day to the white neighborhood where he could not live, to the store he could not own, he grew resentful of his kindly, English-mangling employers. One day he simply stopped going to work.

Wright did not quit without a plan. The United States Post Office hired black men as clerks. To be considered for a job, applicants had to take an exam, which tested their knowledge of the Chicago area and their memorization skills. Wright took the test in the spring of 1928 and waited to see whether he would be hired.

LEARNING AND EARNING

That summer Wright learned that he had passed the exam and was hired for a temporary job at the Chicago post office. He was happy. He worked an eight-hour shift, either during the day or during the night. The schedule gave him plenty of free time to read and write. In Chicago, unlike Memphis, Wright could check out library books under his own name, without a white person's help.

Wright took his reading and writing very seriously. He loved novelists who belonged to what was known as the school of realism. Their stories illuminated the everyday lives and problems of powerless people, and the writers did not shy away from harsh depictions of the seamier side of life. He read Joseph Conrad, Thomas Hardy, and D. H. Lawrence. He especially liked Russian author Fyodor Dostoevsky, whose stories portrayed the oppression the common people of Russia experienced under the czars' rule. Wright was methodical in his reading. "I would read all of a writer's books before passing on to another," he explained.

With the earnings from his post office job, Wright could afford to bring his mother and brother to Chicago. They all lived together in cramped quarters, and Wright had no privacy. But he had achieved his goal: he had moved his family out of the South.

SEARCHING FOR STORIES

At the end of the summer of 1928, Wright's temporary post office job ended. He wanted a permanent position, but first he had to pass a physical exam. Applicants had to weigh at least 125 pounds (57 kilograms)—and Wright did not. He stuffed himself with milk and meat to bring up his weight, but he could not make up for a lifetime of undereating. He failed the physical exam. He got a job in a café and over the winter ate as much as he could, looking ahead to the next post office exam in the spring.

In March 1929, twenty-year-old Wright reached the 125-pound (57 kg) mark and passed the physical. While waiting for a permanent job, he was hired at the central Chicago post office as a mail sorter and substitute clerk.

Before he turned twenty, Wright had left the South to live in Chicago and devote himself to writing. This photo was taken in Chicago in 1928.

Once again Wright improved his family's standard of living. Food was plentiful. The family moved to a larger four-room apartment. Finally he enjoyed the privacy he craved. He worked nights and devoted time during the day to his reading and writing.

At this time Wright mostly wrote short stories. Although he spoke "standard" English, he wanted his writing to capture the feel and experience of the ghetto. He filled pages with efforts to depict black speech patterns. He wrote and wrote but was not satisfied with his efforts. What his stories lacked, he believed, was a connection to the real workings of society. He did not yet have solid ideas about the world that could be expressed in his writing.

"I FELT BLEAK"

While Wright was waiting for a post office job to open up, the nation was changing in ways that dashed his hopes for an orderly life of eight-hour workdays and nights of reading and writing. In 1929 the U.S. economy started to go into an economic depression. As business slowed down, people used the mail less. With less mail to handle, the post office needed fewer clerks and mail sorters. Wright's hours were cut. Then, on October 29, 1929, the prices of stocks sold on the New York Stock Exchange plummeted, ushering in the economic catastrophe known as the Great Depression.

At first Wright did not think the stock market crash would affect him much. Like millions of other Americans, however, he found his life dramatically altered by the depression. By the spring of 1930, the post office no longer needed his services.

Many Americans lost their jobs during the Great Depression. Breadlines like this one in Chicago were common.

The Great Depression

The Great Depression began on October 29, 1929, the day when companies' stock prices on the New York Stock Exchange fell dramatically. The depression affected all Americans. Banks closed because they had lost money that they had invested in the stock market. People who had put their money in banks were left without funds.

A vicious cycle gripped the nation. People could not buy as many goods and services as they once had. Without customers, businesses lost money. Without money, businesses could not provide jobs. And without jobs, people could not afford food, furniture, clothing, heating fuel, or rent.

Those who were poor before the stock market crash were left with nothing. Landlords threw out residents who could not pay rent. People slept in parks and picked food out of trash cans. Charitable organizations tried to help, but the U.S. government did not yet have a strong system for helping people in need. The effects of the depression—millions of people out of work and a slowdown in business and manufacturing activity across the country—continued for more than a decade.

Wright got a lucky break that summer when he was rehired for part-time work, but in the fall he was out of a job again.

Through it all, Wright continued writing. He started a novel—which he called *Cesspool*—that drew on his experiences working at the post office. In April 1931, *Abbott's Monthly*, a magazine with a black readership, published one of Wright's short stories, called "Superstition." The suspenseful story was not the serious literature Wright was striving to produce, but he did celebrate his first fiction sale. Unfortunately, *Abbott's* ran out of money and shut down before he received his payment.

Wright took whatever temporary jobs came his way. But things only got worse. Leon suffered from stomach ulcers and could not work. Desperately short of funds, the family had to move to a cheaper apartment. "The place was dismal; plaster was falling from the walls; the wooden stairs sagged," Wright later wrote. "When my mother saw it, she wept. I felt bleak. I had not done what I had come to the city to do."

4

Red Days

BY 1932 COOK COUNTY, ILLINOIS—the county in which Chicago is located—had opened offices to distribute food and other assistance to its citizens. Almost half of the African American workers in Chicago could not find jobs. Richard Wright was among them.

One morning Wright walked to an office of the Cook County Bureau of Public Welfare and asked for help. He had hoped he would never have to make this request, but his family needed to eat. After interviewing him, a relief official declared him eligible for food aid. Wright also qualified for one of the jobs the government was creating to put people back to work. Soon he was cleaning city streets. During the Christmas season in 1932, he worked at the post office again. When that job ended in early 1933, Wright got a job digging ditches for Cook County. Next he worked in a laboratory at Michael Reese Hospital in Chicago.

Wright was glad to provide food for his family. He benefited from new work and welfare programs put in place by President

Franklin D. Roosevelt, who took office in March 1933. Wright accepted the government's welfare. But he did not think those benefits made up for an unfair and oppressive society.

Three years earlier, enjoying the security of his post office job, Wright had felt his writing lacked purpose. As his fortunes fell, however, his aimlessness also started to fall away. With no economic security, he was forming new ideas about society that would give his writing a target. He was moved by the condition of poor people, no matter what color they were. He thought about what might improve life for the people whose labor drove the nation but who had little control over their destinies. His ideas soon showed up in his writing.

"YOU ARE NOT ALONE"

To some Americans, the depression proved that the U.S. economic system was broken. They wanted to replace capitalism, the system of private ownership of property and businesses, with Communism. Communism depended on a powerful central political party to make economic decisions for the nation and to control all businesses, as well as the government. Communists had held power in the Soviet Union since 1917, and they promoted Communist movements in other countries, including the United States.

Organizers formed the U.S. Communist Party in 1919. Although the party's ultimate goal was to overthrow the U.S. economic and political system and install a Communist system, the leaders knew that a Communist revolution would not happen overnight. They reached out to U.S. workers to help them with their workplace problems. They told the workers that the hardships they suffered under their bosses would disappear in a Communist system. Communists made a special point of recruiting black Americans, recognizing the unfair discrimination

Wright was drawn to the U.S. Communist Party partly because of its activism against racism. Whites and blacks alike attended meetings like this one in the early 1930s.

blacks faced in many aspects of American life. The party also courted intellectuals and writers, promoting Communism as the best means to achieve the economic and social justice that many of them advocated.

Wright agreed with the Communists that the U.S. economic system exploited the masses of ordinary workers. He appreciated that the U.S. Communist Party stood strongly against racism. The Communists formed a legal organization to fight white racist terror groups such as the Ku Klux Klan. In 1931, when nine young black men had been accused of attacking two white women in the "Scottsboro Boys" case in Alabama, the Communist Party had helped to expose the charges as bogus and racially motivated. To Wright, the Communists seemed like the only political group that cared about justice for black people.

In the fall of 1933, a friend from Wright's post office days, Abraham Aaron, urged him to come to a meeting of a new organization. It was the Chicago chapter of the John Reed Club, a Communist Party group for writers and other artists. The club was named for John Reed, a famous American Communist journalist. Not expecting much, Wright showed up at the meeting in downtown Chicago. There he found men and women, nearly all white, who took writing seriously. To Wright's surprise, they respected his thoughts and his potential as a writer.

John Reed (above) *was a well-known journalist from Oregon who wrote an eyewitness account of the 1917 Russian revolution titled* Ten Days That Shook the World.

Capitalism vs. Communism

Under capitalism, private companies and individuals own and control business enterprises. Some individuals get wealthy, while others do not. Under Communism, a single political party holds power, making both political and economic decisions.

When the Great Depression occurred, only one country in the world, the Soviet Union, had adopted a Communist system. Soviet Communists had come to power after a bloody revolution in Russia in 1917.

Communist organizations in other countries, including the Communist Party of the United States of America (CPUSA), took direction from the Soviet Union. Their goal was eventual revolution against capitalist systems around the globe.

During the depression, Communists blamed U.S. capitalism for the widespread hardship. The Americans who embraced Communism believed that it offered a better way to divide wealth among all people. Membership in the CPUSA increased during the depression. Many prominent writers and thinkers, including John Dos Passos and Theodore Dreiser, embraced some Communist principles. Their involvement in Communist conferences and publications helped the party attract attention. By 1939 CPUSA

Theodore Dreiser

membership peaked between 50,000 and 75,000. This was only a tiny percentage of the U.S. population, which was nearly 131 million in 1939.

By the 1930s in the Soviet Union, membership in the Communist Party was not open to the masses, but instead was limited to people who were approved by various Communist committees. Communist Party officials received better food, housing, travel privileges, and education than ordinary people. Shortages of goods were common. Under the leadership of Joseph Stalin, the Soviet Communists outlawed most private property, clamped down on all dissent, and brutally stifled individual freedoms. To rid himself of political rivals, Stalin ordered the persecution, imprisonment, and murder of thousands of his fellow Soviet Communists. His bloody and repressive dictatorship caused many American Communists to turn away from the Communist Party.

Joseph Stalin

Wright left the meeting with an armful of magazines published by the Communist Party and other radical and left-wing organizations that shared the Communists' ideas. In the articles and stories, he found an acceptance of the black experience as part of the shared life of the working class. "It did not say, 'Be like us and we will like you, maybe,'" he later wrote. "It said, 'If you possess enough courage to speak out what you are, you will find that you are not alone.'"

Wright liked what he read. But he also found the stories unrealistic. The Communists had a notion, often pictured in art, of muscular workers holding red banners (the color red symbolized Communism), leading masses of angry people ready to overthrow the bosses, the government, and the entire capitalist system. Wright's experiences told him that the real world was not like that. He did not think Communists would attract followers—especially black followers—with this vision of active revolution.

In the real world, Wright believed, poor people felt angry, but they also felt powerless. It would not be easy to stir them into a revolutionary fervor. He formed a goal. Through his writing, Wright would create bridges between Communists and ordinary people. He would write in plain language about the lives of people at the bottom rung of society, and he would hold out the hope that they could break free of their oppression by banding together.

A POET EMERGES

Inspired by his idea, Wright wrote some poems. He used free verse—poems that do not rhyme or have a regular pattern, or meter. He showed them to his friend Abraham Aaron and another Communist writer, Bill Jordan. Both men reacted positively. They said they would publish two of the poems in the John Reed Club magazine, *Left Front*. They would submit a third poem, "I Have Seen Black Hands"—which they considered the strongest—to *New Masses*, the leading left-wing literary magazine in the United States.

Wright's first two published poems appeared in the January–February 1934 issue of *Left Front*. The poems were called "A Red Love Note" and "Rest for the Weary." In June 1934, *New Masses* published "I Have Seen Black Hands." Although *New Masses* was affiliated with the U.S. Communist Party, many Americans with an interest in literature and the arts read the journal. Leading writers and critics, white and black—including Ernest Hemingway, Thomas Wolfe, Dorothy

Wright's first two published poems can be seen listed in the contents page of the January–February 1934 issue of Left Front, *a publication of the John Reed Club.*

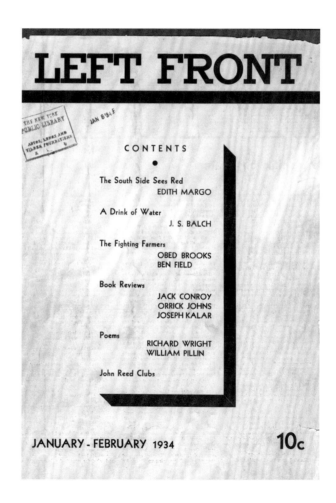

LEFT FRONT

CONTENTS

The South Side Sees Red
EDITH MARGO

A Drink of Water
J. S. BALCH

The Fighting Farmers
OBED BROOKS
BEN FIELD

Book Reviews
JACK CONROY
ORRICK JOHNS
JOSEPH KALAR

Poems
RICHARD WRIGHT
WILLIAM PILLIN

John Reed Clubs

JANUARY - FEBRUARY 1934   **10c**

Parker, Erskine Caldwell, Theodore Dreiser, and Langston Hughes—published stories, essays, and poems in *New Masses*. For an unknown writer such as Wright, getting published in the journal was a major accomplishment.

Wright wrote more poems with revolutionary themes, and leftist journals published them. On the strength of his poetry, Wright became well known on the left-wing literary scene. The Chicago John Reed Club elected the twenty-four-year-old writer to a leadership position. And he joined the U.S. Communist Party. Wright finally was part of a group of people who, like himself, were outsiders in society and wanted to fight injustices.

African American poet and novelist Langston Hughes was one of many leading writers of the 1930s attracted to the ideals of Communism.

Although Wright found kindred spirits among the writers in the U.S. Communist Party, his emphasis on writing set him apart from other Communist Party activists who were more interested in politics. Many black Communists in particular did not trust Wright, because he was a writer and read books that had not been approved by U.S. Communist Party leaders. They mocked his proper speech. "He talks like a book," one member said. Wright also liked to dress conservatively, in suits and ties, and other black Communists made fun of him.

Wright's difficulties with some Chicago Communists did not harm his social life, however. He dated several women who were in the John Reed Club or who were sympathetic to Communist or leftist causes. The John Reed Club, where Wright met many of his friends, had a nearly all white membership, and Wright did not hesitate to date white women. He had romances with black women as well.

LUCK AND LITERATURE

In the summer of 1934, as his literary status was rising, Wright lost his job at the hospital. Poetry did not pay for food and rent, and for a while he went back to sweeping streets and digging ditches. Soon this work dried up as well.

Short of funds, Wright moved his family to a small apartment next to the railroad tracks. Then he got lucky. County officials assigned him to work at the South Side Boys' Club. The club was built to keep black boys in the ghetto from getting into trouble. When not working at the boys' club, Wright wrote and did volunteer work for the John Reed Club and the U.S. Communist Party.

Wright continued to compose poetry. He also wrote short stories. In "Big Boy Leaves Home," a group of black teenage boys goes swimming. The pleasant outing turns horrifying after a white woman sees the young men drying off, naked, on the banks of the whites-only creek in a Southern town. The woman's fiancé goes after the boys with a gun. He kills two of them before the protagonist (main character), Big Boy Morrison, kills him. Big Boy and the other surviving teenager, Bobo, flee. Overnight, a white mob with dogs tracks down Bobo and murders him. Big Boy escapes and is rescued by a black truck driver who takes him north to Chicago.

Wright worked on two other stories, "Down by the Riverside" and "Long Black Song," at the same time. These also portray black men struggling in a racist world. In all three stories, Wright's black characters are far from model citizens. The teenagers in "Big Boy Leaves Home" skip school to go on their swimming adventure. In "Down by the Riverside" and "Long Black Song," black protagonists kill white men. Wright showed that racism has damaged these characters. Of course they are angry and act badly, the stories insist—look at how the characters have to live.

Wright shared his work with a circle of literary friends, including John Reed Club members Joyce and Ed Gourfain and Jane and Herbert Newton. Evenings at the Newton or Gourfain home often centered on Wright reading his latest efforts. His friends gave their reactions and suggested he read the works of other authors who shared his fascination with the complexity of human experience—such as T. S. Eliot, William Faulkner, James Joyce, Gertrude Stein, Marcel Proust, and e. e. cummings. Wright also became interested in sociology, psychology, and history.

TASTE OF NEW YORK

In the fall of 1934, U.S. Communist Party leaders announced that the John Reed Clubs would be shut down. The decision reflected the Communists' new focus on fighting fascism—the militaristic ideology that had taken hold in Italy under dictator Benito Mussolini and in Germany under Adolf Hitler. Although the U.S. Communist Party still rejected capitalism, its leaders saw fascism as a greater immediate threat. Since the John Reed Clubs did not directly aid in this fight, the leaders wanted to dissolve them.

Wright spoke out against the decision, which he believed slighted young writers like himself. His outspokenness alienated many of his fellow Chicago Communists. Nonetheless, Communist literary magazines continued to showcase his writing. And the party tapped Wright to travel to New York City as a delegate to the Communists' first American Writers' Congress. Party members wanted to hold him up as an example of the Communists' openness to black Americans.

The writers' congress opened at Carnegie Hall on April 26, 1935. Wright not only spoke before the congress but also was asked to help lead the League of American Writers, a new Communist group.

During his week in New York City, Wright was reminded that no matter how much his Communist comrades accepted him, much of the rest of white America did not. The congress organizers had failed to get Wright a hotel room. After the first sessions, he went from one part of the city to another, looking for a hotel that would accept a black man. The only place he found to stay was a Negro Young Men's Christian Association (YMCA).

Still, Wright enjoyed his first trip to New York City. The U.S. Communist Party had attracted some of the nation's most famous writers to the congress. Attendees included the novelists Theodore Dreiser, John Dos Passos, Erskine Caldwell, and James T. Farrell; poet Langston Hughes; and journalist Meridel Le Sueur. Wright was thrilled to rub elbows with these literary greats. He felt at home with the New York Communists he met. Except for his difficulty finding a place to stay, he also felt at home in New

York City. He liked the busy streets, the vibrant Broadway theaters, and the possibilities the city seemed to hold for a writer.

"IT'S GOT TO BE WORTHWHILE"

But Chicago was still Wright's home, and he returned there to
start a new job that he had arranged before his trip to New York.
One of the agencies President Roosevelt created to fight the
nation's continuing joblessness was the Works Progress
Administration, or WPA. The WPA created government-funded
jobs, including work for writers through the Federal Writers'
Project (FWP). Wright got a job as a supervisor with the FWP. His
task was to help research and write a history of Illinois. Project
administrators encouraged him to report on the experiences of
black people in Chicago as part of the book.

*Many of the jobs created by the Works Progress Administration
(WPA) in the 1930s used manual labor to build new roads, parks,
and other public projects and facilities.*

It was a plum job. Earning a regular salary, Wright moved his family out of their squalid rooms by the railroad tracks to a better apartment on the South Side. He got to know other African American writers who worked at the FWP and its sister agency, the Federal Theatre Project. These writers included poet and novelist Margaret Walker, poet Gwendolyn Brooks, novelist Arna Bontemps, and playwright Theodore Ward. Wright and other black writers were at the center of a vital new cultural community in Chicago that brought together and encouraged African American writers, musicians, and scholars.

Wright continued to publish poems in left-wing magazines. One of his best-known poems appeared in July 1935 in *Partisan Review*, a journal started in 1934 by John Reed Club members. Titled "Between the World and Me," the poem described a lynching. Its closing lines contain an unsparing depiction of the victim's murder:

> And my skin clung to the bubbling hot tar, falling
>   from me in limp patches. . . .
> Then my blood was cooled mercifully, cooled by a
>   baptism of gasoline.
> And in a blaze of red I leaped to the sky as pain
>   rose like water, boiling my limbs. . . .

In January 1936, Wright submitted his short story "Big Boy Leaves Home" to the *New Caravan*, a collection of contemporary writing. The editors accepted the story and mailed him a fifty-dollar check as payment. Fifty dollars was more than a week's salary for a post office clerk in 1936. Wright was less successful with his novel, *Cesspool*, which several publishers rejected.

When the *New Caravan* anthology was published later in the year, reviewers at major publications such as the *New York Times*, *Saturday Review of Literature*, and the *New Republic* singled out

*Wright began to attract a wider literary
audience in 1936.*

Wright's story for special praise. Some said it was the best story in
the entire book. This marked the first time Wright's talents drew
notice from the non-Communist literary world.

In the world of Chicago Communists, however, Wright faced
criticism. Local Communist Party leaders pressed him to show
his dedication by participating in political work. They convinced
him to organize a protest against the rising cost of living. He was
required to hold meetings about problems in the Chicago housing market. Wright resented every minute of these assignments.

By 1937, the Federal Writers' Project in Chicago was facing
budget cuts. Wright looked around for steady work and took the

post office examination—again. And once again, he scored high. "I got a letter saying I had been given a full-time job in the post office," he recalled later. "It meant $2,100 a year [equivalent to almost $30,000 in current dollars]. I took that letter, sat on my bed, and thought it out."

He tore up the letter. Wright needed to escape the stifling clutches of the Chicago Communist Party. He was ready for change in other ways as well. He had enjoyed publishing success, but he wanted more. He thought that living in New York City might lead to greater exposure in the publishing world. So, on a Friday afternoon at the end of May 1937, Wright said good-bye to his coworkers at the Federal Writers' Project.

"I want my life to count for something," he explained to one of his friends, writer Margaret Walker. "I don't want to waste it or throw it away. It's got to be worthwhile."

Wright's clothes, books, and typewriter fit into a single suitcase. He bade his family farewell and headed east.

5

New York New Horizons

WRIGHT TRAVELED TO NEW YORK BY CAR, hitching a ride with friends. When he arrived in the city, he stayed with other friends until he found a cheap place to live in Harlem. He joined a local Communist Party group so he could be hired as a writer for the party's newspaper, the *Daily Worker*. Stationed in the paper's Harlem bureau, Wright wrote dozens of articles. Most focused on day-to-day matters such as political meetings, protests, and living conditions in Harlem. The writing did not stimulate him, but it paid the rent.

At the same time, Wright published articles that did reflect his passions, especially about racism and writing, in other journals. Although he was a cordial and soft-spoken man, he expressed his views plainly and sometimes harshly in his writing. In October 1937, Wright condemned fellow black Southerner Zora Neale Hurston, attacking her new novel *Their Eyes Were Watching God*. "Miss Hurston *voluntarily* continues in her novel the tradition which was *forced* upon the Negro in the theatre, that is, the minstrel technique [performances featuring crude skits and songs meant to be comical, portraying demeaning stereotypes of African Americans] that makes the 'white folks' laugh," he complained in a review in *New Masses*. He added that Hurston's black characters were "quaint" and their lives "safe and narrow."

Wright insisted that black authors convey a social or political message. In "Blueprint for Negro Writing," an essay published in November 1937, he dismissed much of the work of black writers who came before him. Wright argued that these authors tried to appease white readers, who viewed the black writers as "French poodles who do clever tricks."

NEW CHALLENGE
A Literary Quarterly

| VOLUME II | FALL 1937 | NUMBER II |

CONTENTS

EDITORS
DOROTHY WEST   MARIAN MINUS

ASSOCIATE EDITOR
RICHARD WRIGHT

CONTRIBUTING EDITORS: Sterling Brown, Collins George, Robert Hayden, Eugene Holmes, Langston Hughes, Russell Marshall, Loren Miller, Arthur Randall, Margaret Walker.

NEW CHALLENGE: Published quarterly, 25c a copy; $1.00 a year. Copyright 1937 by Dorothy West. No reprint may be made without permission of the editors. Make all checks payable to NEW CHALLENGE, 371 West 117th Street, N. Y. C.

"Blueprint for Negro Writing" was published in the Fall 1937 issue of New Challenge, *for which Wright was also the associate editor.*

LIKE A JAZZMAN

If Wright sounded sure of himself and his ideas, it was because he was. "He had the kind of confidence that jazzmen have," Ralph Ellison wrote. "He was well aware of the forces ranked against him, but in his quiet way he was as arrogant in facing up to them as was [famous jazz musician] Louis Armstrong in a fine blaring way." Wright and Ellison met in 1937, soon after Wright arrived in New York. Five years younger than Wright, Ellison was just beginning to think about writing as a career. After being introduced by poet Langston Hughes, Ellison and Wright became good friends.

Wright met Ralph Ellison in 1937. Ellison is best known for writing Invisible Man. *He is pictured here in 1964.*

Wright maintained his confidence even as the mail brought rejection letters. Publishers turned down both *Lawd Today*, a revised and renamed version of his novel *Cesspool*, and another novel, *Tarbaby's Dawn*, based on Wright's experiences as a teenager in the South. Editors explained that though his fiction may have been a realistic portrayal of black life in America, readers could not handle so much bleakness and violence.

Wright did not back away from his views. In autumn 1937, he gathered four of his short stories, including "Big Boy Leaves Home," in a collection and submitted them to a contest held by *Story*, a prestigious literary journal. In December the magazine's editor told Wright that he had won first prize.

This came as a sweet triumph for the twenty-nine-year-old writer. Contest judges chose his work out of six hundred entries. One of the stories—"Fire and Cloud"—was chosen for publication in *Story* magazine. In Wright's story, a black church leader is caught between his poor parishioners who need welfare assistance and white officials who refuse to help them. Under the rules of the contest, the magazine offered the entire collection to the publishing house Harper & Brothers, which accepted it for publication as a book. The first prize award was five hundred dollars, the largest sum Wright had ever earned. When the award was made public in February 1938, Wright told a reporter he planned to treat himself to a new suit and a big steak dinner.

The *Story* prize not only meant that Wright could eat well for a while. It also made his name known beyond his small literary circle. He approached a well-regarded literary agent, Paul Reynolds, and asked him for help placing other work with publishers. Reynolds took on Wright as a client and negotiated a contract with Harper & Brothers for the sale of Wright's next novel— which he had yet to write. Wright's editor at Harper & Brothers was Edward Campbell Aswell. He was white and Southern and, to Wright's amazement, completely respectful toward him.

Wright had a good relationship with his editor at Harper & Brothers, Edward Aswell.

NO MORE UNCLE TOMS

Things were happening quickly. Suddenly articles about Wright appeared in newspapers, and he was interviewed on the radio. In the spring of 1938, his story collection came out under the title he had chosen for it, *Uncle Tom's Children*. With this title, Wright signaled that black people—his characters—would not quietly accept oppression. They would not be "Uncle Toms," an insulting term for blacks who meekly accepted white superiority. This new generation would fight back.

The book drew glowing reviews. Even Eleanor Roosevelt, wife of President Franklin Roosevelt, praised the book in her regular column for the *New York World-Telegram*. She said it was "beautifully written and so vivid that I had a most unhappy time reading it."

Some white reviewers questioned the stories' harsh portrayal of white people, and some black reviewers did not like Wright's depressing portraits of black people. One of the most negative reviews came from Zora Neale Hurston, whose own novel Wright had denounced the year before. "This is a book about hatreds," she wrote in the *Saturday Review of Literature*. "Not one act of understanding and sympathy comes to pass in the entire work."

The U.S. Communist Party embraced its newly famous comrade. Party officials celebrated Wright with honors and invitations to speak at meetings and dinners. In May 1938, the Communist journal *New Masses* published Wright's next short story, "Bright and Morning Star," about heroic black Communists in the South.

CREATING BIGGER THOMAS

Even as the U.S. Communist Party embraced him, Wright was escaping from its payroll. Around the time he won the *Story* prize, Wright quit his job writing articles for the *Daily Worker* to take a position that had opened up with the New York Federal Writers' Project. He was assigned to research and write a section about Harlem for a guide to New York. He worked on other books as well. Because he was an established writer, Wright was allowed to work from home. He could spend time on his own writing while collecting a government salary.

Wright was working on the new novel he had promised Harper & Brothers. The novel centered on a character named Bigger Thomas, a black teenager in a Chicago slum. In crafting this story of despair, crime, and race, Wright drew on his work at the South Side Boys' Club in Chicago in 1934.

At the boys' club, Wright reflected, he had met many Bigger Thomases—black teens with nowhere to go and nothing worthwhile to do, because white society excluded them. "They were paying me to distract Bigger with ping-pong, checkers, swimming, marbles, and baseball," he later explained, "in order that he might not roam the streets and harm the valuable white property which adjoined the Black Belt [the black South Side]. I am not condemning boys' clubs and ping-pong as such; but these little stopgaps were utterly inadequate to fill up the centuries-long chasm of emptiness which American civilization had created in these Biggers."

LIKE DIGGING DITCHES

During the summer and fall of 1938, Wright worked steadily on his novel. "Just as a man rises in the mornings to dig ditches for his bread, so I'd work daily," he said later. Around this time, he broke off a romance with his Harlem landlady's daughter, a poorly educated young black woman, and moved to Brooklyn, one of New York City's boroughs. There his friends Jane and Herbert Newton, who also had moved to New York from Chicago, gave him a room in their home.

Most mornings Wright rose early and walked to a nearby park, with a pad of paper. It had to be a yellow pad. Like many writers, he had developed some quirks as part of his writing process. He returned to the house for a late breakfast, after Herbert Newton had left for work. Wright liked to discuss the book with Jane Newton, who often offered suggestions. In an early draft, for example, after Bigger murders a young woman named Mary Dalton, Wright had him cut off her head with a kitchen knife. Jane pointed out that this was unrealistic—a kitchen knife could not cut off a human head.

When Wright disagreed, Jane coaxed him into performing an experiment. She gave him a kitchen knife and a butchered

Wright moved into a room in the home of his friends Jane and Herbert Newton in New York. The Newtons are pictured here in 1934 with one of their children.

chicken (which she was going to cook) and told him to cut off the chicken's neck. He could not. The knife was not sturdy enough. In the next draft, Wright wrote an ax into the scene, and Bigger uses that to decapitate Mary.

Before he finished his first complete draft, Wright chose a title: *Native Son*. With this title, Wright suggested that Bigger Thomas was a product of the U.S. political and social system. He became a criminal not because of some outside or foreign influence, but because of the hatred and neglect of his own native country. Once Wright finished the first draft, he sent it to Paul Reynolds for comments and immediately began revising the manuscript himself.

MORE MILESTONES

Although Wright remained preoccupied with *Native Son* into 1939, it was not his only focus. He met and seriously dated two different women. One was Ellen Poplar, a white Communist Party activist from Brooklyn who shared Wright's passion for fighting injustice. The other was Dhimah Rose Meadman, a modern-dance teacher of Russian background. He fell in love with the lively and intelligent Poplar, but she hesitated to marry him because her family opposed interracial marriage. Hurt, Wright turned to Meadman.

Wright celebrated other literary milestones in 1939. In the spring, he received a Guggenheim Fellowship, an award granted to exceptional artists and scholars. The fellowship was intended to allow him to write for a full year, with no other work obligations. He received twenty-five hundred dollars, more than twice his salary at the Federal Writers' Project. He resigned from the project and, though he was still revising *Native Son*, started work on a new novel about black women.

Still, he devoted much of his attention to *Native Son*. While working on his second draft of the novel, Wright developed a system that he adopted for all his writing projects. He typed out the changes he wanted to make, then cut up the paper so that he could glue his additions to the latest version of the manuscript. His floor became a mosaic of papers as he arranged and rearranged his edits. Wright hired a typist to retype his cut-and-pasted pages into a clean manuscript. Then he could start cutting, typing, and pasting all over again.

One night in June 1939, Wright decided his manuscript was ready. He gathered the Newtons and some neighbors and read from the novel. The next day he gave the manuscript to his editor.

While Wright felt good about his story and his message, he felt less sure about how the public and his publisher would receive the book. "Really, I don't believe that they are going to publish it," he wrote to his friend Margaret Walker back in Chicago.

BOOK CLUB BUZZ

Wright did not have to worry. Edward Aswell, his editor at Harper & Brothers, loved *Native Son*. He edited the book quickly and submitted it to the Book-of-the-Month Club, the nation's top mail-order bookseller. Each month the club offered its members a recommended book—the "book of the month." Being selected for this honor guaranteed book sales and created a buzz throughout the literary world.

With the intense work of writing the novel behind him, Wright turned to a personal matter. In August 1939, in a tiny ceremony at a Harlem church, he married Dhimah. The couple, along with her son from a previous marriage, soon found a house together in Crompond, a suburb of New York City.

Wright married Dhimah Rose Meadman in August 1939.

Native Son

For many white readers, *Native Son* provided their first understanding of the hopelessness, horror, and hatred spawned by racism. Early in the novel, Bigger Thomas voices his anger about how white people treat black people: "They don't let us do *nothing*. Every time I think about it I feel like somebody's poking a red-hot iron down my throat. . . . We live here and they live there. We black and they white. They got things and we ain't. They do things and we can't. It's just like living in jail. Half the time I feel like I'm on the outside of the world peeping in through a knothole in the fence. . . . They own the world."

Through a welfare office, Bigger gets a job as a driver for a rich white family, the Daltons. They are liberal people and do not consider themselves racists—yet they own some of the worst black slums in Chicago. On his first day, Bigger is told to drive the Daltons' beautiful daughter, Mary, to a university class in the evening. When Bigger reports for duty, however, he finds that the rebellious girl has plans to go out on the town with her Communist boyfriend, Jan Erlone. Mary and Jan try to treat Bigger as an equal, which he finds uncomfortable. They have him take them to a club in the ghetto and sit with them. Bigger's discomfort grows.

Afterward, Bigger drops Jan off and takes Mary home. She is so drunk that she can't climb the stairs to her room, so Bigger must carry her. In her bedroom Mary clings to Bigger, apparently making sexual advances. Just then, Mrs. Dalton, who is blind, enters the room. Bigger puts a pillow over Mary's face to quiet her. He knows that if he is found in a white woman's bedroom, the consequences will be serious. He holds the pillow tight over Mary's face, releasing it when Mrs. Dalton leaves the room—only to find that he has suffocated the young woman.

Bigger panics. He gets rid of Mary's body by cutting it up and putting it in the Daltons' furnace. He hatches a plan to pretend Mary has been kidnapped. He involves his girlfriend in his plot, and when she does not cooperate, he kills her too.

Bigger is soon arrested and put on trial. His defense lawyer, a Communist, argues to the court that Bigger's life circumstances led him to commit his crimes. But Bigger is sentenced to death by electrocution. Bigger reflects on his actions when he learns of his death sentence. "When a man kills, it's for something," he says. "I didn't know I was really alive in this world until I felt things hard enough to kill for 'em."

A honeymoon would have to wait, however. Wright was too busy getting *Native Son* ready for publication. Among other things, he had to deal with the Book-of-the-Month Club. The judges were interested in making *Native Son* their monthly selection. They were willing to take a risk and offer a novel by a black author, but they drew the line at some graphic passages of sex and violence, which they believed might offend readers. The judges asked Wright to rewrite these scenes. He did, and *Native Son* became the March 1940 Book of the Month. It was the first novel by a black author to achieve that distinction.

This advertisement for Wright's novel Native Son *emphasizes its selection as the Book of the Month.*

6

A Literary Phenomenon

NATIVE SON WAS PUBLISHED on March 1, 1940. Ecstatic reviews soon followed. The *New Yorker* magazine declared, "Richard Wright's *Native Son* is the most powerful American novel to appear since [John Steinbeck's] *The Grapes of Wrath*." More glowing reviews appeared in the *New Republic*, *New York Times*, *New York Post*, *Newsweek*, and *Time*. Many reviewers called Wright the leading social critic of the day.

Thanks in part to such favorable reviews, the book sold by the tens of thousands. Some bookstores ran out of copies just hours after displaying them for sale. In fewer than three weeks, *Native Son* sold more than 200,000 copies. No Harper & Brothers book had sold as well in twenty years. And the book kept selling, rising to the top of best-seller lists across the country. Wright was the first black author in U.S. history to write a best seller.

Congratulations poured in from friends and strangers. The novel's success also brought him money. He bought a house back in Chicago for his family. He bought himself some new clothes.

He was not rich, but he could stop worrying about his next pay-check for a while.

Newspapers, radio shows, and lectures featured the young writer. People wanted to know more about this thirty-one-year-old African American with the violent imagination. What they

Native Son *drew a lot of attention when it was released, as shown by this large advertisement from the Books section of* the New York Times.

learned was that he was genial, good-looking, and serious about his writing. "I sweat over my work," he told the *New York Sun*. "I wish I could say it just flows out, but I can't. I usually write a rough draft, then go over it, page by page." In the same article, he confided that he enjoyed movies and that to relax, he sometimes saw as many as three a day. He also liked to develop his own photographs.

MEXICAN INTERLUDE

Wright and his wife, Dhimah, needed a quiet change of scenery after the hullabaloo surrounding *Native Son*. In late March 1940, just three weeks after the novel's publication, the couple traveled to Cuernavaca, a city in south-central Mexico known for its mild weather. They had postponed a honeymoon after their wedding the previous summer. Now Wright and Dhimah set off by ocean liner for Mexico—but they were not alone. Dhimah's two-year-old son, her mother, and her pianist traveled with them.

The family settled into a large villa in a community of Americans called Miraval Colony. The house had a swimming pool, lush gardens, and ten rooms. The contrast with the slums of Wright's youth could not have been greater, and he enjoyed his surroundings and Cuernavaca's warm springtime weather.

One of the things that most impressed Wright was the racial tolerance he observed in his new surroundings. "I write from a country—Mexico—where people of all races and colors live in harmony and without racial prejudices or theories of racial superiority," he wrote in the *Atlantic Monthly* in June 1940.

But his time in Cuernavaca was not quite as enjoyable as Wright had hoped. While one sunny day melted into the next, letters brought upsetting news from home about *Native Son*. Sales were tapering off at about 250,000 copies. And the honeymoon of positive reviews was over.

Criticism bubbled up in the black press and in Communist journals. Black reviewers expressed concern that the first best-selling book by a black author featured an antisocial black protagonist. Communist reviewers complained that the poor black people Wright portrayed in his story did not fight the white power structure.

While Wright responded as best as he could from a distance, he faced problems in his Cuernavaca villa as well. There, too, the honeymoon was over. Wright found life with his new wife disagreeable. He sought solitude and simplicity, but she preferred socializing. He wanted his wife to consider his needs first, but she had a strong personality and her own ideas about marriage. Wright concluded that they were incompatible.

In June 1940, Wright headed back to the United States alone. His marriage was falling apart. He had not made much progress on his new novel, *Little Sister*. But he had not wasted his time in Mexico. He had written a long essay called "How 'Bigger' Was Born" for the *Saturday Review of Literature*. He had traveled into the surrounding countryside with novelist John Steinbeck and a film crew working on Steinbeck's movie, *The Forgotten Village*. And he had decided to accept an offer by Orson Welles and John Houseman, both experienced actors and directors, to adapt *Native Son* for the stage.

RESTLESS FEET

Wright looked forward to starting afresh with new projects. He would coauthor the *Native Son* stage script with Paul Green, an award-winning playwright. Wright had also signed on to write the text for a book of photographs about African American life and culture.

Rather than go directly back to New York, Wright decided he wanted to revisit his roots and travel through the South. He got a quick reintroduction to Southern ways at the border between Mexico and Texas, where a white official called him "boy," used racial slurs, and took his U.S. passport away without explanation. (A passport is a travel document issued by governments that identifies citizens and provides them with legal protections while traveling in foreign countries.) Wright sat in a Jim Crow railcar on the train to Mississippi. In his hometown of Natchez, he visited his father and other relatives. Wright's father, Nathan, was working as a farm laborer again. In his ragged overalls and with his gnarled hands, he seemed far from the ogre of Wright's childhood.

Wright (center) *stands with his father, Nathan Wright* (second from left) *and three other men during a visit to the South.*

Leaving Natchez, Wright rode another segregated train to North Carolina to meet with playwright Paul Green. After a few days, Wright headed to New York, with promises to return for a more in-depth writing session.

Dhimah Rose Meadman was also back in New York, spending time with writer Ralph Ellison and his wife. Ellison had been best man at Dhimah and Wright's wedding less than a year earlier. Meadman may have hoped that Ellison could help her and Wright reconcile, but for Wright, the marriage was over.

Wright stayed in New York for only a few days before boarding a train to Chicago. There he conducted research for his new book on African American life. In contrast to his degrading experiences while traveling in the South, in Chicago Wright

Wright (kneeling) *sets up a shot with the help of an assistant while doing research in Chicago in 1940.*

The Harlem Renaissance and Beyond

As the first best-selling African American author, Richard Wright was a literary trailblazer—but many black writers before him had prepared the way. Beginning in the early 1900s, and especially in the 1920s, African American writers gained national prominence in an outpouring of literature and art about the black experience in America. This period became known as the Harlem Renaissance. (Some scholars prefer other terms, such as "Negro Renaissance" or "New Negro Movement.")

Poet, essayist, and playwright Langston Hughes—whom Wright had met in 1935 at a writers' conference in New York—was among the most famous of these black writers. Novelist Zora Neale Hurston also preceded Wright. Many other influential writers contributed to the flourishing of black literature that began before Wright entered the literary stage. They included poets Countee Cullen, James Weldon Johnson, and Claude McKay; novelist Nella Larsen; and editor and activist W. E. B. DuBois.

was treated like a celebrity. He signed books at the American Negro Exposition, an event celebrating the seventy-fifth anniversary of emancipation.

Wright's restless feet next took him back to Chapel Hill, North Carolina, where Paul Green taught at the University of North Carolina. Through weeks of a heat wave in July and August 1940, Wright and Green worked on *Native Son*. By the time Wright left for New York in mid-August, the two men had produced a working draft of the play. They had also surprised more than a few

Wright works with Paul Green (left) *on the play* Native Son *in Chapel Hill, North Carolina, in July 1940.*

passersby who, through a window in a university building, saw what was at that time an amazing sight: a white man and a black man hovered over a typewriter, the pages of their efforts spread across a table.

DRAMA OFFSTAGE AND ONSTAGE

Back in New York, Wright moved in again with his friends Jane and Herbert Newton in Brooklyn. He worked on further revisions to the play. He revised his novel *Little Sister* and wrote book reviews. He read history books for the book project on African

American life. Then one day Ellen Poplar came to visit the Newtons. Poplar and Wright immediately reconnected. It was love—at second sight. This time they both were ready and able to say yes to marriage.

Wright and Poplar got married on March 12, 1941. The newlyweds set up housekeeping in a small apartment in Manhattan. Poplar, now Mrs. Wright, learned Southern-style cooking to please her husband. Wright continued his practice of writing in the mornings. He took a lunch break with his wife. In the afternoons and evenings, the Wrights saw friends, went to the movies, attended U.S. Communist Party or other meetings, or went to the library or for a walk.

Wright and his second wife, Ellen Poplar, were married in 1941.

Two weeks after the Wrights' marriage, *Native Son* opened on Broadway at the St. James Theatre. New York theater critics gave the play respectful reviews. The drama tested the limits of racial tolerance by showing physical contact between a black man and a white woman. It also broke new ground in its portrayal of black people as multifaceted human beings, rather than as servants or clowns. "We're making history in the theater," said Canada Lee, the boxer-turned-actor who played Bigger Thomas. "The Negro has never been given the scope that I'm given in this play."

Above: *Wright* (left) *talks with Canada Lee* (center) *and Orson Welles, the star and director, respectively, of the Broadway production of* Native Son.

Left: *A playbill from the original Broadway production of* Native Son

Native Son played for almost three months at the St. James Theatre, until June 1941. The producers had hoped for a longer Broadway run, but attracting large audiences to such a challenging play proved difficult. On the road, the production did well, selling out in many theaters.

VOICES OF HISTORY

Wright did not travel with the play. He was busy collaborating with photographer Edwin Rosskam on *12 Million Black Voices*, the folk history of African American life. Wright's text was not long—only four chapters—but he worked hard on it, rewriting until his words reflected not only the facts but also the feelings he wanted. The book traced the slaves' voyages from Africa, life in the South,

Shown here is the cover of 12 Million Black Voices, *Wright's collaboration with Edwin Rosskam.*

and the Great Migration of black people to the North. Wright's text read almost like poetry, with an intimate feeling.

"Each day when you see us black folk upon the dusty land of the farms or upon the hard pavement of the city streets, you usually take us for granted and think you know us," the book began, "but our history is far stranger than you suspect, and we are not what we seem." Wright displayed a sense of irony in sentences like this: "The immemorial stars must have gazed down in amazement at the lowly of England and Europe who, with hearts full of hope, pushed out to sea to urge rebellion against tyranny and then straightway became engaged in the slave trade, in the buying and selling of our human bodies."

In the fall of 1941, *12 Million Black Voices* was published to positive reviews. Ralph Ellison told Wright that "the book makes me feel a bitter pride; a pride which springs from the realization that after all the brutalization, starvation, and suffering, we have begun to embrace the experience and master it. And we shall make of it a weapon more subtle than a machine gun, more effective than a fighter plane!"

7

Looking Inward

RALPH ELLISON HAD MACHINE GUNS and fighter planes on his mind in 1941 for good reason. World War II was raging in Europe. Germany, under the control of Adolf Hitler and the Nazi Party, had taken over practically all of Europe, from Czechoslovakia and Poland in eastern Europe, to Belgium and France in western Europe. The German army was marching through the Soviet Union in an attempt to conquer that country as well. Italy and Japan joined with Nazi Germany in an alliance known as the Axis.

Wright believed that the United States should not get involved in the war. Since 1940 he had been active in a group that shared this opposition, the Communist Party's American Peace Mobilization. In Wright's view, the war concerned European countries battling over extending their power and feeding their capitalist economies. To Americans who argued that the United States should enter the war to preserve democracy in Europe, Wright countered that Americans needed to promote democracy at home by fighting racism. Wright also objected to segregation in the U.S. armed forces, which gave black soldiers the least desirable jobs.

Wright expressed his views in an article called "Not My People's War." After Nazi Germany invaded the Communist Soviet Union, however, the Communist view of the war flip-flopped immediately. Wright, however, remained opposed, and this created tension between him and the U.S. Communist Party.

Wright's stance changed after December 7, 1941, when Japan attacked the United States naval base at Pearl Harbor, Hawaii. Like most Americans, Wright agreed that the United States had to respond to the attack and join the war in Europe as well. Although Wright supported his country as it entered the war, he did not want to turn his back on the fight against racism at home. He expected the U.S. Communist Party to challenge race discrimination in wartime employment, but the party was more interested in winning the war against Germany than in criticizing U.S. policies. Wright wanted the party to stand for individual rights and freedoms, and he found that it did not. Dismayed, Wright quietly but decisively left the Communist Party. Ellen Wright, who had been even more active in the party than her husband, joined him.

A WRITER'S LIFE

As he had before the war, Wright spent his days living a writer's life. At the end of 1941, he was working on two novels. Leaving behind *Little Sister*, his novel about black women, he took a strand of that story and wove it into a new novel titled *Black Hope*. It told the story of well-to-do black people who live in a nice house in Brooklyn by masquerading as the white homeowners' servants. Wright's agent Paul Reynolds found it interesting but in need of revision.

On the Bandstand

In one of his most unusual projects, Wright took up a friend's challenge to write lyrics for a blues song in 1941. As his subject, he chose the great boxing champion Joe Louis. Famed bandleader and composer Count Basie set the words to music. In October 1941, Wright attended a recording session in which the renowned black singer and actor Paul Robeson sang Wright's song "King Joe" with the Count Basie Orchestra. The record went on sale the next month and sold forty thousand copies in three months.

Wright talks with Count Basie (left) *at a recording session in 1940.*

Wright also wrote a new novel, *The Man Who Lived Underground*, about Fred Daniels, a black man who is stopped by police on his way home from work. The police accuse him of murder and try to get him to confess by beating him. After the police hang him by his feet, Daniels signs a confession. He soon escapes, runs into the street, and jumps into a manhole. He finds himself in the underground world of sewer tunnels—and stays there to live. Wright was pleased with *The Man Who Lived Underground*, but both his agent and his editor at Harper & Brothers rejected it. Wright reworked it as a novella, which did get published in a magazine.

On April 15, 1942, Wright became a father when Ellen gave birth to a daughter, Julia. At age thirty-three, Wright was young enough to be drafted into service in the armed forces. The government exempted him for the time being, however, since he provided the sole financial support for his family, including his mother.

SPEAKING TRUTH

For some time, Wright had been casting about for a writing project that would get him back in the bookstores. He was struggling with his novels. He published articles and reviews in magazines, but he really wanted a book project. However, he lacked a subject or story that was important to him and would interest readers— or at least interest his agent and editor.

Early in April 1943, Wright joined a friend, Chicago sociologist Horace Cayton, on a trip to Fisk University in Nashville, Tennessee. Fisk was one of the oldest black colleges in the United States. Both men were invited to speak to students, faculty, and community members. Wright was not sure what approach to take. Finally he decided to speak informally about his experiences and his problems as a black American writer.

The speech shocked his audience. Wright later told a newspaper reporter what happened:

> I gave a clumsy, conversational kind of speech to the folks, white and black, reciting what I felt and thought about the world; what

I remembered about my life, about being a Negro. There was but little applause. Indeed, the audience was terribly still, and it was not until I was half way through my speech that it crashed upon me that I was saying things that Negroes were not supposed to say publicly, things that whites had forbidden.

After the speech, audience members, black and white, stayed behind to speak with Wright. One black educator told him he was the first person to speak the truth in Nashville. Students plied him with questions about his life. Wright had struck a chord among blacks and whites, young and old. He saw the power in the story of his personal struggle against racism. Wright had his book project.

PASSING JUDGMENT

Back in Brooklyn, Wright got to work. Sometimes he wrote for ten hours at a time. He recounted his days of hunger as a child and the stark environment in which he lived. He wrote about his family, his neighbors, the white people he met, and the white people he never met but who ruled his world. Wright described his gradual awareness of race discrimination and the humiliations and injustices he and other black people suffered. He also did not flinch from unflattering observations about the black community and his family. In Wright's story of his upbringing, the black people in his life discouraged his interest in reading and writing, beat him, and insisted that he quietly submit to the racist system.

Wright's goal was not strictly to write an autobiography but an account of his life—particularly his childhood—that would say something about the lives of all black people in the South. He explained: "I wrote the book to tell a series of incidents strung through my childhood, but the main desire . . . was to render a judgment on my environment. . . . That judgment was this: the environment the South creates is too small to nourish human beings, especially Negro human beings." Wright believed he was not just writing about himself. He did not describe some events with complete accuracy. He changed some details to present a larger picture.

In the middle of this intense undertaking, Wright, his wife, and their baby daughter moved to a six-room apartment in Brooklyn Heights. In the new apartment, Wright set up a comfortable study for himself and his six hundred books. And he kept writing until he had finished his book. He called it *American Hunger*. On December 17, 1943, he sent the manuscript to his agent and waited for a response.

Wright reads to his daughter, Julia, in their New York apartment in the 1940s.

Wright did not have to wait long. A week later he received a telegram from Paul Reynolds: "YOUR AUTOBIOGRAPHY IS ENTHRALLING."

Edward Aswell, Wright's editor, agreed. The manuscript covered Wright's life through 1937, the year he left Chicago for New York. Aswell suggested that the book focus only on Wright's life as a child and teenager in the South. The rest of the story, he thought, would work better in a separate book or article. Aswell sent the manuscript to the Book-of-the-Month Club. The club decided to make Wright's latest book a featured selection.

Even though the book ended with Wright's journey out of the oppressive South to the less racially divided North, the story was not optimistic or uplifting. Fleeing the South was an act of self-preservation, but the North did not offer a haven. The North simply presented a different face of racism. Dorothy Canfield Fisher, an author and influential Book-of-the-Month Club judge, asked Wright to consider ending the book on a hopeful note—to acknowledge that some white Americans, at least, were trying to help solve America's race problem.

But Wright could not soften the book's tone and remain true to himself. As he explained in a letter to Fisher, "I do not think that Negroes will be treated any better in this country until whites themselves realize that there is something dead wrong with the American way of life." Fisher respected Wright's views and did not press further.

Just before the book was printed, Wright himself requested one more change. He wanted the title to be *Black Boy*. "Now, this is not very original, but I think it covers the book," he wrote to Aswell. "It is honest. Straight. And many people say it to themselves when they see a Negro and wonder how he lives." The book was set for publication in early 1945 under Wright's chosen title, *Black Boy: A Record of Childhood and Youth.*

FBI Target

At his publisher's suggestion, Wright had cut the sections about his years in Chicago from *Black Boy*. Even before *Black Boy* appeared on bookstore shelves, however, Wright sold the story of his time as a young Communist in Chicago to *Atlantic Monthly* magazine. Titled "I Tried to Be a Communist," the article came out in August 1944. In it Wright criticized party leaders who valued conformity and loyalty above individuality.

Despite this public announcement of Wright's split from the Communist Party, the U.S. government still viewed him as a dangerous left-wing radical. The Federal Bureau of Investigation (FBI), the government agency that investigates people who might be harmful to national security, had first begun keeping tabs on Wright after publication of *12 Million Black Voices*. At that time, the FBI was concerned that Wright's hostility toward the U.S. government might endanger the war effort. In addition, although the United States and the Communist Soviet Union were allies during World War II, the U.S. government viewed American Communists as threats. FBI agents started investigating Wright and filing reports on his activities.

FBI agents studied Wright's essay "I Tried to Be a Communist" and decided that he still needed monitoring. His articles, an FBI memo noted, "indicate a complete disapproval . . . of the American way of life." In fact, the memo continued, Wright was even more "radical and militant with respect to the advancement of the Negro" than the U.S. Communist Party was. Wright would not have disagreed.

THE "NEGRO WRITER"

Wright was eager to take on new projects. He came up with a wide range of ideas. In 1944 he wrote scripts for radio programs about a fictional black family. He envisioned a series called "Sunny Side of the Street." He thought it held promise, but no radio station wanted to produce the show.

Wright also tried to sell an outline for a screenplay that he wanted to write, called "Melody Unlimited." It would tell the story of Fisk University's Jubilee Singers, who introduced traditional African American music—"slave songs" and spirituals—to widespread audiences starting in the late 1800s. Wright could not interest filmmakers in the project, however. His plans in 1944 for a book of photographs and text documenting the experience of children in Harlem, and for a collection of essays by black writers, also failed.

These setbacks took a toll on Wright. In January 1945 he wrote in his journal, "This gloomy but sunlit afternoon I've been wondering how I can ditch the literary life and start anew at something else. . . . I wish I could make films. Or engage in some sort of government work. I know that as long as I live in the United States, I can never change my profession, for I'm regarded fatally as a Negro writer, that is, as a writer whose ancestors were Negroes and therefore the Negro is my special field."

INSTANT BEST SELLER

As Wright questioned his life path, *Black Boy* was published in March 1945. Thanks in part to advance sales by the Book-of-the-Month Club, a strong publicity campaign, and favorable early reviews, the book made the best-seller lists immediately. With its negative outlook and harsh language, *Black Boy* challenged readers. Predictably, some white critics objected to the book's language and its dismal view of white Southerners.

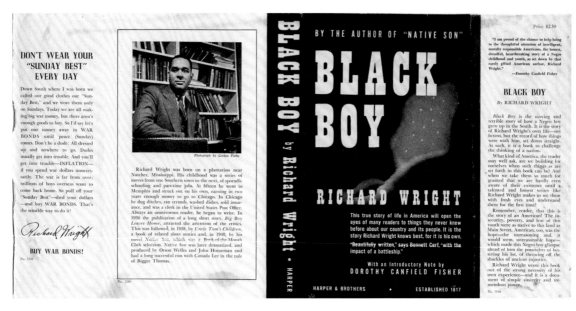

Black Boy *became a best seller when it was released in 1945. The jacket of the first edition is shown here.*

Some black readers and critics found Wright's picture of Southern blacks degrading. One passage in particular aroused controversy among black readers: "I used to mull over the strange absence of real kindness in Negroes, how unstable was our tenderness, how lacking in genuine passion we were, how void of great hope, how timid our joy, how bare our traditions, how hollow our memories, how lacking we were in those intangible sentiments that bind man to man and how shallow was even our despair."

The statement struck many black readers as harsh and insulting—and utterly wrong. They were taken aback and hurt that Wright had passed judgment on black communities, culture, and values.

Wright did not back away from his assertions, but he tried to explain why he wanted to show the negative aspects of black life. In an interview with *PM* magazine in April 1945, he referred to the "legend" that "all Negroes are kind and love animals and children."

He explained, "That legend serves to protect certain guilt feelings about the Negro. If you can feel that he is so different that he is just naturally happy and he smiles automatically you kind of exclude him, in an ironic sense, from the human race and therefore you don't have to treat him exactly like you would treat other people and you don't have to feel bad about mistreating him." Black people are human beings, Wright said, and when human beings are oppressed, their personalities and communities change for the worse.

Despite the criticism, *Black Boy* had many champions—and many readers. The book reached number one on the nation's leading best-seller lists in the spring of 1945, and it remained in the top ten for most of the year. By the end of 1945, *Black Boy* ranked fourth in sales among all nonfiction books for that year in the United States. More than 500,000 copies had been sold—twice as many as *Native Son* and a new record for a black American author.

8

Between Two Worlds

BLACK BOY INSTANTLY EXPANDED Wright's fame. His voice was heard on the radio across the country. His face appeared in *Life* magazine. Hundreds of readers sent him fan letters. People filled auditoriums to hear him speak.

Wright's fame had a flip side. Along with fan mail, he received hate mail. Some people sent angry letters to the FBI asking the government to ban *Black Boy* and ship Wright off to fight on the front lines in the war against Japan. (The war in Europe was winding down, but the conflict with Japan in the Pacific Ocean region continued until August 1945.) Some libraries would not put *Black Boy* on their shelves.

LONGING FOR FREEDOM

Wright was the most well-known black author in the United States. His fame extended abroad, too, as his books were translated into other languages and published in other countries.

And yet Wright's fame did not shield him from the racism he faced in daily life. When the Wrights decided they wanted to buy a house in New York City's Greenwich Village neighborhood, they had to use a ruse. Their lawyer created a corporation to buy the property, because real estate agents and banks tried to discourage black buyers. After the sale, the Wrights faced resistance from tenants living in the house, which was divided into several large apartments. White neighbors tried to buy the house so that the Wrights' mixed-race family would not move into the neighborhood. Although the Wrights owned the house by February 1945, they delayed moving in for months, to allow the controversy to settle down.

Wright and his family moved to Greenwich Village in 1945. The New York City neighborhood is known for attracting artists.

Other Voices

Though famous, Wright was not the only celebrated black writer in his time. His friend from Chicago, Margaret Walker, won a prestigious award from Yale University for her 1942 book of poetry, *For My People*. Ralph Ellison, whose writing Wright encouraged when the two became friends in New York in the late 1930s, published stories, book reviews, and articles. He is best known for his novel *Invisible Man* (1952), for which he won the National Book Award in 1953.

Wright's success with *Native Son* and *Black Boy* put him in a position to help other emerging African American writers. In 1945 a friend suggested that Wright meet twenty-year-old James Baldwin. Wright invited the younger writer over for drinks and read the early chapters of Baldwin's first novel. Impressed, Wright helped Baldwin get a grant from a fund recently established by Harper & Brothers, so that Baldwin could afford to keep writing and establish his career. The novel eventually was published as *Go Tell It on the Mountain* (1953). Baldwin published many other books as well, including *Notes of a Native Son* (1955) and *The Fire Next Time* (1963).

Wright also encouraged writer Chester Himes by publishing a favorable review of his first novel, *If He Hollers Let Him Go* (1945). Himes wrote many more novels and became best known for a series of detective novels set in Harlem. About the same time, Wright helped boost the career of Chicagoan Gwendolyn Brooks, whose poetry earned her the first Pulitzer Prize won by a black writer, in 1950. Brooks went on to have an award-winning career as a poet, novelist, and children's writer.

Other incidents prevented Wright and his family from fully enjoying his success. When he tried to buy a country home in Vermont, the seller stopped dealing with him once she discovered he was black. And although Wright lived in Greenwich Village, he could not find a single barber in his neighborhood willing to cut a black man's hair. He had to travel to Harlem to get a haircut.

Wright had long dreamed of visiting Europe, especially France. He admired French writers such as Marcel Proust, who had written an influential seven-volume set of novels, translated as *Remembrance of Things Past*, or *In Search of Lost Time*, before he died in 1922. Wright was also interested in modern French thinkers, including Jean-Paul Sartre, Albert Camus, and Simone de Beauvoir. They were leaders in existential philosophy, a school of thought that addresses the meaning of human existence and freedom. Existentialism emphasizes individual free will, rather than conformity to society's rules.

African American writers and artists who had lived in France before World War II said they had not experienced racial hostility there. Wright longed to live somewhere he could feel completely free. He had left the South years ago in search of that environment, and he was willing to leave the country for it.

After the publication of *Black Boy*, Wright began corresponding with American writer Gertrude Stein, who lived in Paris. Stein encouraged his interest in traveling to France. He and Ellen decided to go to Paris, with Julia, for a long visit.

To travel abroad, however, Wright needed a passport. A U.S. official had taken Wright's old passport when he returned to the United States after his trip to Mexico in 1940. He applied for a new one, but the government responded slowly. At the time, Americans had to get approval from the U.S. government before traveling to Europe, which was still suffering from the devastations of the recent war. The FBI and other agencies knew that Wright was a radical. They feared he would vent his feelings about American racism while in France. Spurred on by Gertrude Stein, the French government extended Wright and his family an official invitation to help Wright obtain the necessary permission from the U.S. government. Finally, just three days before he planned to depart, the U.S. State Department gave Wright the documents he needed—but he had to fly to Washington, D.C., to get them.

NOT A BLACK PROBLEM

On May 1, 1946, Wright, Ellen, and Julia left New York onboard the SS *Brazil*. "Already," Wright wrote to Ralph Ellison from the ship, "the harsh race lines of America are fading."

Gertrude Stein encouraged Wright to travel and to write. She is most well known for writing The Autobiography of Alice B. Toklas.

Arriving in the French port of Le Havre a week later, the Wrights immediately noticed the wreckage from the recent war. They saw ruined buildings everywhere. The Wrights boarded a train to Paris, where they were greeted as dignitaries. Stein met their train at the station, Gare Saint-Lazare.

Searching for Wright at Saint-Lazare was Maurice Nadeau, a critic and writer who was reporting for the French publication *Combat*. Nadeau spotted Wright playing with little Julia on the platform. The Frenchman described the thirty-seven-year-old American writer: "His eyes are animated behind his metal-rimmed eyeglasses. He takes off his hat showing his kinky hair cut short. His daughter interests him more than I do."

Although Wright did not have time for a proper interview during his first minutes in Paris, when Nadeau asked him whether the "black problem" in the United States was nearing a solution, Wright responded. "There is not a black problem in the United States, but a white problem," he said. Humor lit up his eyes. Wright's quip was printed in other publications.

That first morning in Paris, driving from the train station to a hotel, Wright delighted in the city's beauty. Buildings, boulevards, and gardens had been spared the wartime devastation. Apart from the city's physical beauty, Wright enjoyed its welcoming atmosphere. Paris officials named him an honorary citizen. After three weeks in France, he told a reporter that he had "not detected the least iota of racial tension against the Negroes."

Wright spent much of his time attending parties and receptions held in his honor. He gave lectures and met with writers and editors. He took French lessons. He participated in the launch of *Présence Africaine* (African Presence), a magazine created by French-speaking intellectuals with roots in France's African colonies. (At the time, France held colonial power over more than a dozen African nations, including Algeria, Tunisia, and Senegal.) This project sharpened Wright's interest in the

African struggle for independence from French and other European colonial rule.

Wright's political interests also shifted during a trip to London, where he met more nonwhite writers from Africa and Asia. He became good friends with George Padmore, a black intellectual who was born in Trinidad (then part of the British West Indies). Padmore was helping lead a worldwide movement to bring independence to European colonies in Africa. Wright became fascinated by the problem of how Europe's African and Asian colonies could become independent. His concern for blacks expanded to include millions of Africans and Asians.

Wright (left) *stands with Dorothy and George Padmore, who opened his eyes to the struggles of minorities all over the world.*

While in France, Wright thought he would work on his long-standing novel-in-progress, *Black Hope*, but he found little time to write. He did, however, make time to talk with the press. In interviews he spoke frankly about what he viewed as a nearly impossible racial situation in the United States.

Wright did not try to hide his pessimism about race relations in America. Yet his interviewers consistently noted his mild demeanor. On the surface, he seemed neither angry nor unhappy. Wright closed one interview with a doleful assessment of Americans, but then he smiled. His interviewer wrote, "At this point, Richard Wright smiled a smile that contradicted the pessimism of his pronouncements. . . . And when he laughed, one could not imagine that anyone who laughed in that way was not, at bottom, a firm optimist."

Much as Wright detested the racism in the United States, he did not plan to move permanently to Paris. Wright worried that his life in France did not give him time to write. Ongoing shortages in Europe, including a housing shortage in Paris, made daily life inconvenient. By the fall of 1946, the Wrights decided they would return to New York, where their new home in Greenwich Village awaited them.

INTO EXILE

On January 11, 1947, the Wright family sailed back to New York on the passenger ship *Queen Mary*. Their first task was to settle into their three-story house on Charles Street in Greenwich Village. Ellen enjoyed decorating, while Wright arranged his library.

A 1947 magazine article described the Wrights' new home: "The gray-walled, freshly painted living room had pictures stacked in the mauve [purple] fireplace, a suitcase in one corner and a linen press full of towels at one side, but otherwise the chairs, desk and sofa were neatly arranged." As Wright unpacked,

Wright poses on the steps of his Greenwich Village house in 1947.

he laughed with the reporter and talked about the difference between France and the United States. "[A] Negro isn't a Negro in Paris," Wright said. "He's just another Frenchman." Yet, Wright continued, he needed to live in the United States. "My main job is in this country. I'd like to visit there often, but I belong here. No, I was fashioned in this peculiar kind of a hell." He laughed when he said that.

But laughter could not make the "peculiar kind of a hell" any easier to endure. Although life in New York offered material comforts lacking in postwar Paris—abundant food, reliable plumbing, ample clothing on store shelves—Wright found it uncomfortable in other ways. With the war over and an alliance with the Soviet Union no longer necessary, the U.S. government took a harsher stance toward Communist and left-wing critics. Wright also bristled at what he perceived as Americans' undue emphasis on money and consumer goods.

But what bothered him most was the continuing race discrimination. On the streets of Greenwich Village, Wright and Ellen received unfriendly stares and comments. Some restaurants showed hostility toward black patrons by serving them coffee with salt in it. Local grocers and store owners called Wright "boy." And he had to think about his five-year-old daughter, Julia, too. One day a department store clerk refused to allow Julia to use the restroom. Wright could not bear the thought of his little girl being treated as less than equal to anyone else.

Neither his freshly painted, comfortable house nor his fame could make up for the racism that seeped into Wright's daily life in New York. So he and Ellen changed their minds. They would not stay in America after all. They sold their Greenwich Village house. They bought a big Oldsmobile and Wright learned how to drive. And on July 30, 1947, the Wright family boarded a ship to cross the Atlantic Ocean once again. This time they had no plans to return to the United States. Payments from the sales of *Black Boy* would support the family until Wright published another book. Traveling on the SS *United States* with the Wrights were seventeen trunks of possessions, the Oldsmobile, and their new black-and-white cat, Knobby.

AN AMERICAN ABROAD

Wright left the United States because he found life there too painful, but France was no paradise. Shortages of food and household goods continued to be a problem in Paris. The electricity frequently went out. And the Wrights could not find a suitable apartment in Paris. The family moved from one place to another. On top of the unsettled living arrangements, in the fall of 1947 Wright fell sick for weeks with a flulike illness. He wrote very little.

But Wright was busy. He gave lectures about his writing, especially after the French translation of *Black Boy* won a prestigious French literary award in January 1948. Wright's fame in Europe grew when theaters in London, England, and Prague, Czechoslovakia, put on his play *Native Son* and when *Black Boy* was translated into more languages. Newspapers and magazines interviewed him and asked him to write articles.

During his first year in Paris, Wright spent hours with Jean-Paul Sartre and Simone de Beauvoir, two of France's leading thinkers and writers. From talks with Sartre and others, Wright

Wright (right) *became interested in existentialism through talks with Simone de Beauvoir* (center) *and Jean-Paul Sartre.*

became interested in existentialism. For Wright this focus led him to become more devoted to fighting injustice and standing up for what he believed. In 1948, with Sartre, Wright became involved in a left-wing French group that wanted Europe to stay neutral in the developing cold war between the United States and the Soviet Union. This conflict—referred to as "cold" because it mainly involved words, economics, and spying rather than weapons—arose after World War II. The cold war divided major nations of the world into two hostile camps: the Communist, pro-Soviet side and the capitalist, pro-United States side.

Wright believed that neither of the superpower nations—the United States and the Soviet Union—stood for true individual freedom, and neither had the right to control other countries.

PARISIAN DAYS

In May 1948, the Wrights moved for the third time in eleven months. This time, however, they found a place to call home. The apartment on rue Monsieur le Prince was in the Latin Quarter, an area with an artistic atmosphere similar to Greenwich Village. The apartment took up an entire floor of a building. Wright had a large, comfortable study. Julia attended a nearby school, and the neighborhood abounded with cafés frequented by writers and artists, including Americans (known as expatriates, or "expats").

The Wrights entertained a steady stream of visitors. A close friend, American political cartoonist Oliver Harrington, later noted, "It was a huge, rambling old-fashioned apartment. . . . This was the apartment to which came the great, the not so great, and those who would never be great. All were welcome." In January 1949, the Wrights welcomed a new addition to their home—a second daughter, named Rachel.

Although Wright's novel writing was bogged down, he tried to establish a working routine. He usually sat down at his

Underwood typewriter by seven in the morning and worked until two in the afternoon. Then he went out, often to a favorite bookshop and on to a gathering place for writers and American expats, such as the Café Tournon.

Not everybody welcomed Wright into the expatriate community. Communists considered him a traitor. Anticommunists did not like him any better. The U.S. government even employed agents in Paris to keep track of Wright, whose highly public criticism of the United States was considered an embarrassment. And in the spring of 1949, James Baldwin, who was also living in Paris, published a widely read magazine article called "Everybody's Protest Novel." In his essay, Baldwin criticized *Native Son*. He called it a failed protest novel because it presented a stereotype—Bigger Thomas—instead of a fully human protagonist. Wright was deeply wounded by Baldwin's charge, and fellow writers took sides in the feud that developed between the two men.

BIGGER ON THE BIG SCREEN

Wright felt restless and eager to do something different. The opportunity came from a French film producer, Pierre Chenal, who wanted to make a movie of *Native Son*. Chenal asked Wright to write the screenplay. Somewhat more surprisingly, Chenal also wanted Wright to play Bigger Thomas. Wright was forty years old—more than twenty years older than the adolescent character of Bigger. Wright also had no acting experience. Still, he accepted Chenal's offer.

In August 1949, with work on the movie script well under way, Wright boarded an ocean liner headed to New York. From there he traveled to Chicago, where a film crew shot city scenes to use in the movie. Then it was back to New York to board the SS *Uruguay* to Buenos Aires, Argentina. Chenal had spent much of World War II in Argentina and decided to film most of *Native Son* there. While at sea on the *Uruguay* for three weeks, Wright followed a strict diet and worked with a fitness trainer to try to regain the slim physique of a young man. He lost thirty-five pounds—but neither diet nor exercise could make him look like a teenager. Between filming and traveling, Wright did not return to Paris until August 1950.

Wright (left) *works out with his trainer aboard the S.S.* Uruguay *to lose weight for his role as the much-younger Bigger Thomas.*

Native Son opened in Buenos Aires on March 30, 1951. Despite Wright's clumsy acting, the film received excellent reviews and showed to packed movie houses throughout Argentina. Wright looked forward to similar success in the United States. But first the movie had to pass through the New York Board of Censors. Censorship boards like this one determined whether films were morally upstanding and suitable for the public. The censors raised many objections. They did not want audiences to see Mary and Bigger kissing, and they did not want to hear Bigger's lawyer (a Communist) defend Bigger by denouncing the United States. The censors cut thirty minutes from the movie, shaving it down to just over an hour.

Communists Jan Erlone (Gene Michael, seated, middle) *and Mary Dalton* (Jean Wallace, right) *take Bigger Thomas* (Richard Wright, left) *to a nightclub in this still from* Native Son. *Censors objected to the relationship that developed between Bigger and Mary.*

The 1951 movie poster for Native Son *emphasized the violence that is at the center of the story.*

When *Native Son* opened in New York on June 16, 1951, critics panned the film. They noted that the acting was poor and the required cuts gutted the story. Although the film played in several states, censors in Ohio, Pennsylvania, and Wisconsin banned it. Wright saw the censored version of his movie in July in Paris and felt sick. It was a failure, at least in the United States.

INSIDE THE OUTSIDER

Life in Paris was becoming less enjoyable for Wright. He called for the world's nations to resist aligning with the superpowers in the cold war, but he saw the tentacles of American influence everywhere. The French government, he believed, pandered to the

United States. Back in the United States, Senator Joseph McCarthy publicly accused government officials and private citizens of taking part in a Communist conspiracy to undermine the nation. For Wright, the expatriate community in Paris no longer seemed like a group of independent thinkers. Americans abroad were choosing sides between East (the Soviet Union) and West (the United States). Wright refused to choose. While others shared his views, his stance isolated him in the American community.

By 1952 Wright had not published a book in seven years. He decided to work again on a novel he had abandoned years earlier. To focus his attention, he took a small apartment in London at the beginning of the year and wrote steadily for three months. By spring he had a 650-page manuscript. Its main character was Cross Damon, a black man, but its central theme was not racial. Rather, the book reflected Wright's interest in existential philosophy. Damon struggles as much with the meaning of life as with racial discrimination. Like many of Wright's earlier works, the story involved several murders.

Wright's agent did not love the book, called *The Outsider*, but he thought it would sell. Harper & Brothers accepted the novel. When it was published in March 1953, reactions were mixed. *Jet* magazine wrote, "Wright still displays his terrific gifts for writing brilliantly. But his almost psychopathic lust for violence gets the better of him . . . and his story becomes as completely phony and unreal as a cheap drugstore whodunit." Some reviews were much harsher. *Commentary* magazine declared the book "very boring." Critics suggested that Wright did not measure up to two other leading black writers, James Baldwin and Ralph Ellison—both of whom had benefited from Wright's advice and help as they launched their careers.

Wright had expected poor reviews, so the reception to *The Outsider* did not take him by surprise. The book still sold fairly well, though it never climbed into the top ten of U.S. best sellers.

Wright holds a copy of The Outsider, *which was published in 1953. The book sold fairly well but was not critically acclaimed.*

He had already completed another novel, called *Savage Holiday*, featuring a white protagonist whose strange relationship with his mother drives him to kill another woman. His agent did not care for it, but a paperback publisher accepted it.

Wright did not dwell on the bad reviews for *The Outsider*. By 1953 *Black Boy* had sold more than 900,000 copies and *Native Son* nearly 600,000. And Wright had a new project he was excited about. He was going to Africa.

9

Looking Outward

WRIGHT'S INTEREST IN AFRICA had been growing ever since he became friendly with George Padmore in the 1940s. Padmore had become an adviser to Kwame Nkrumah, who was leading the British colony of the Gold Coast toward independence. In 1952 the African-born Nkrumah became prime minister of the Gold Coast, which Great Britain had granted limited power to govern itself. (The colony did not gain full independence until 1957, when it became the free nation of Ghana.) Wright was fascinated by the African colony's route to political independence and by the issues raised as a tribal culture moved toward modernity. He wanted to spend time in the country and write about his findings.

Paul Reynolds, Wright's agent, agreed that this was a stimulating idea. Harper & Brothers gave Wright a book contract and money to help pay for his trip. The voyage would mean still more time away from his family, but he and Ellen had gotten used to this pattern. She was developing her own career as a literary agent.

Wright went to Liverpool, England, to board the *Accra*, which set sail for the Gold Coast on June 4, 1953. He was the only American on a ship full of African and English people. The *Accra* reached the port of Takoradi on June 16. Wright had prepared a speech to deliver upon arrival. He was, after all, an internationally known author of African descent. Reporters often flocked to him for interviews when he arrived in a new place. But when Wright stepped off the ship in Takoradi, the crowds simply went about their daily business—and no reporters awaited him.

Prime Minister Nkrumah had sent a friend to meet Wright at the dock. The man helped Wright catch a bus to Accra, the capital. It would take eight hours to travel 170 miles (274 kilometers). Just hours into this new land, Wright already felt overwhelmed by the heat and humidity. Looking out the bus window, he took in the

Wright found himself uncomfortable with the traditional tribal cultures he encountered in West Africa.

view along the route—mud shacks, crowded markets, thick forests. The sight of naked children playing and topless women doing their chores in villages made him feel strange. Africa was going to be more mysterious to him than he expected.

In Accra Wright tried to keep an open mind about aspects of life that differed from his own, but it was not easy for him. The traditional religious beliefs and practices—some of them raucous and even violent—bewildered him and sometimes offended him. He could not get used to nudity among women and children.

Many of the Africans he met laughed at his comments and questions. This struck Wright as socially inappropriate and backward, though the Africans were likely reacting to what they considered his unseemly directness. Yet when an African man asked

Wright took this photograph of an African marketplace on his trip to the Gold Coast, which later became the independent nation of Ghana.

him a question—inquiring what part of Africa Wright's ancestors came from—he could not answer because he did not know. The African was shocked, and Wright was irritated.

Wright did not adjust well to the Gold Coast's climate and the spicy foods. He suffered from an upset stomach and frequently felt feverish and tired. In his journal, he confided his desire to go home. But he had a project to complete. On August 3, he set out to explore the interior countryside. He rented a car and hired a driver. Wright visited villages, met a tribal queen, dined with the king of the Ashanti people, wrote thousands of pages of notes, and took photographs. He stayed as long as his stamina and money would permit. He had thought he might stay in Africa for as long as six months. Instead, on September 2, he headed back home after just ten weeks.

AFRICAN INSIGHTS

Back in Paris, Wright started writing a book about his impressions of West Africa. He worked on it throughout the fall and winter and sent it off to Reynolds in March 1954. Reynolds liked it. Edward Aswell had taken a job at another publishing house, but Wright's new editor at Harper & Brothers accepted it.

Wright's report on his visit to the Gold Coast, called *Black Power: A Record of Reactions in a Land of Pathos*, came out in September 1954. The book related Wright's highly personal, unvarnished impressions of the many things he found strange about the Gold Coast. He wrote of smells and sights that distressed him, of beggars with diseased legs, of blind men with empty sockets where their eyes should have been. He described the mirthless laughter that he found so off-putting. He wrote about women's naked breasts and about tribal rituals he considered primitive.

Wright did not see himself as disrespectful toward traditional African ways. He simply believed that, for the well-being, prosperity, and freedom of its people, Africa needed to change. He blamed the European colonial powers for the poverty and illiteracy in the Gold Coast. He argued that Europeans had deliberately prevented African culture from progressing to become more modern.

Wright's solution for the Gold Coast was startling for a man who had always championed individual freedom. He proposed that black African leaders needed to provide strong, clear direction—with a military regime, at least temporarily—for the people to break away from tribalism and join the modern world.

Not surprisingly, *Black Power* evoked strong reactions. Wright's idea for a regimented society held in check by a military-style discipline struck many readers as appalling. Some book reviewers objected to his harsh words about Great Britain and other European powers. Some found the book too personal to be useful. Readers in the Gold Coast found *Black Power* offensive. Yet other book critics in the United States and France found Wright's account engaging.

Despite all the attention *Black Power* got, the book did not sell well. Wright was disappointed. But he was already on to his next project.

SOUL OF SPAIN

Years earlier, when Wright had first come to France, writer Gertrude Stein had given him some advice. She said, "Dick, you ought to go to Spain."

"Why?"

"You'll see the past there. You'll see what the Western world is made of. Spain is primitive but lovely. And the people! There are no people such as the Spanish anywhere."

By 1954, with *Black Power* behind him, Wright decided to follow his former mentor's advice and investigate Spain—and, of course, to write a book about it.

Harper & Brothers was interested enough in Wright's idea to give him five hundred dollars to get started. In August 1954, during a stifling heat wave, he drove across the border between France and Spain. He had traded his oversized Oldsmobile for a smaller French car. He went to Barcelona, where the first two people he met took him to a Catholic church to pray. When Wright told the young men that he was not Catholic, they seemed amazed. Their religion meant everything to them. On his first day in Barcelona, Wright had already found one of the main themes of his book: the importance of religion and ritual in Spanish life.

Wright spent three weeks in Spain, traveling nearly 4,000 miles (6,400 km) from Barcelona to Madrid, Córdoba to Seville. At the time, Spain was governed by a dictator, General Francisco Franco. This interested Wright, but he was more interested in the Spanish preoccupation with religion and bullfighting. He

Wright saw the Spanish love of bullfighting and devotion to religious ritual as a means of individual expression under an authoritarian political regime. This is a photo he took while in Spain in the 1950s.

believed that the Spanish people, having no hope of individual freedom under Franco, turned to pageantry and rituals as a means of expressing themselves and feeling alive.

Wright returned to Paris, but he made two more trips to Spain, in November 1954 and February 1955. Toward the end of his third trip, Wright visited Seville to observe the city's elaborate celebrations of Holy Week leading up to Easter. Shop windows featured tiny figurines clothed in white robes with tall, pointy hoods. The hoods reminded Wright of the costumes worn by members of the Ku Klux Klan in the American South.

In Seville, Spain, Wright took this photograph of the city's Good Friday procession. The robes had religious meaning, but they reminded Wright of those worn by the Ku Klux Klan.

BEHIND THE ASIAN CURTAIN

Wright had plenty of notes from his trips to Spain, but for the moment he set them aside. Another part of the world called to him: the Far East. In Bandung, Indonesia, leaders of the twenty-nine independent countries of Asia and Africa were meeting in 1955. Most of these countries were former European colonies, and some were trying to remain nonaligned in the cold war between the United States and the Soviet Union. The twenty-nine nations represented about 1.5 billion people—half the world's population at the time.

Thrilled by the prospect that a unified group of nonwhite nations would take a stand against colonialism and cold war politics, Wright decided he had to go. The only Westerners invited to Bandung were journalists, so Wright signed on as an independent journalist for a Paris-based organization. Without even going home from his latest tour of Spain, he left for Indonesia from Madrid on April 10, 1955. Two days and three airplane rides later, he landed in Jakarta, the capital of Indonesia. Bandung, the conference site, was a few hours' drive into the surrounding mountains.

Wright stayed in Indonesia for three weeks. Although he investigated local customs and politics, he focused on the meeting. He listened to such leaders as Jawaharlal Nehru of India, Gamal Abdel Nasser of Egypt, and Norodom Sihanouk of Cambodia. Chinese premier Chou En-lai also spoke to the conference delegates.

Wright finally returned to Paris in late May 1955. Working long hours, he quickly produced a manuscript about what he had learned at Bandung. Rather than offering a comprehensive report on the conference, he wrote about the importance of race and religion in the developing nations of Asia and Africa. Wright believed that their common racial and religious histories drew people in those countries together to resist domination by either

East or West. He called his book *The Color Curtain: A Report on the Bandung Conference* and sent it to his agent in June 1955.

"I CANNOT LIVE IN AMERICA"

After months of travel, Wright needed a break. He and his family spent July through October 1955 at a small farm he had bought earlier in the year. It was in Ailly, about 45 miles (70 km) from

Ellen Wright (center) *and her daughters Julia* (left) *and Rachel feed chickens on the Wrights' farm at Ailly, France.*

Paris. Wright's country house gave him a haven where he could work away from the bustle of Paris. He also enjoyed the beauty of the countryside and the simple chores of a small farm. He joked to his friend Oliver Harrington that he bought the farm so he could have "a place where I can grow me some potatoes." Besides potatoes, Wright planted corn, peas, and beans, which he enjoyed sharing with his friends back in the city.

During that summer in Ailly, Wright thought seriously about new fiction projects he would turn to after he finished the book on Spain. He wanted to keep growing as a writer, but he also needed to make money. Although sales of *Black Boy* had sustained the Wrights since 1945, those payments were decreasing. He needed to write something that would sell well.

At the suggestion of Edward Aswell, his former editor who now worked at McGraw-Hill, Wright outlined a detailed plan of work. He had two new novels in mind, which he described in a thirty-eight-page letter to Aswell. They were complicated and bloody and reflected his views of American racism.

Wright sent his proposal off in October 1955. Aswell's response was not encouraging. Both he and Wright's agent, Paul Reynolds, thought Wright's ideas about racial problems were outdated. "I have a lot of doubts as to whether a man who has been nine years away from this country can successfully write novels laid in this country," Reynolds wrote to Wright. "America has changed in the last ten years. . . . People's attitudes have changed, dialogues have changed."

Wright had heard this criticism before—that he was out of touch with the strides made in the United States on race relations. But Wright was not convinced that things had improved much. In August 1955, a group of white men in a small town near Greenwood, Mississippi, murdered fourteen-year-old Emmett Till, a black boy from Chicago. Till had allegedly spoken disrespectfully to a white woman while he was visiting relatives in Mississippi.

Perspectives on Progress

By the mid-1950s, Wright's literary agent, his editor, and his critics were suggesting that he had been away from the United States for so long that he could no longer write convincingly about his native land. Wright's ideas about racism were outdated, they said—race relations in American society and politics had changed. Civil rights groups such as the National Association for the Advancement of Colored People (NAACP) and the Congress of Racial Equality (CORE) advocated for equal rights for black people. The U.S. Supreme Court ruled that racial segregation in transportation across state lines violated the Constitution. An executive order outlawed discrimination in federal government jobs. And in 1954, in the case of *Brown v. Board of Education of Topeka, Kansas*, the Supreme Court ruled that segregation in public schools was unconstitutional.

Wright's critics were correct in pointing out that the United States was changing. But Wright was also correct that America had a long way to go before black people would achieve equality. After the Supreme Court ruling against racial segregation in schools, for example, white citizens and political leaders in the South fought desegregation for years. Throughout Wright's life, black people, particularly in the South, were not allowed to vote, get well-paying jobs, or go to whites-only restaurants, motels, parks, and libraries.

Emmett Till sits with his mother, Mamie Bradley, a few years before his murder in 1955.

Before killing Till, the men tortured and disfigured him. In September an all-white jury found the two men arrested for the murder not guilty of the crime.

"That is why I cannot live in America," Wright wrote to a friend in November. "Such wanton killings fill me with disgust, uneasiness, and a sense of dread."

10 The Struggle Ends

THE COLOR CURTAIN, Wright's book on the Bandung conference, received mixed reviews when it was published in March 1956. It did not attract many readers, since most people had little interest in political conferences.

During the first half of 1956, Wright hammered out *Pagan Spain: A Report of a Journey into the Past*. He deliberately chose a provocative title. He had concluded that although Spaniards were immersed in the Catholic religion, their attitudes and practices were closer to paganism—that is, to ancient, non-Christian faiths. With its ritual and superstition, Wright thought, Spain was not really part of the modern Western world.

Pagan Spain came out in February 1957. Not many people bought it. Catholic and Protestant critics alike objected to Wright's blunt assessment of religion in Spain. For example, without much evidence of research, he interpreted certain Catholic rituals as pagan and sexual. While noting the similarity of the Spanish hoods to those worn by Ku Klux Klan members in the

American South, he did not explain the hoods' meaning in Spain—to hide wearers' identity from other people, but not from God, as they repented of their sins in public.

Still, while some readers may have stayed away from *Pagan Spain* because the ideas offended them, many Americans simply were not interested in reading about Spain. Discussing the book in the *Chicago Tribune*, the distinguished black columnist Roi Ottley suggested in March 1957 that Wright could find better outlets for his "gifts and insights as a novelist."

RISING DISCOMFORT

Wright was in fact working on a new novel in early 1957. But he was also involved in another nonfiction project. It grew out of a tour he had taken in Scandinavia—Sweden, Norway, and Denmark—in late 1956. Wright was popular in Scandinavia. His novel *The Outsider* sold well there, and his speeches attracted appreciative audiences. His Swedish publisher wanted to collect his lectures about racial issues in a book. Wright gathered four talks under the title *White Man, Listen!* He also sent the book to Edward Aswell, who had moved to the Doubleday & Company publishing house. Aswell was impressed with the collection and accepted it for publication. *White Man, Listen!* appeared in American bookstores in October 1957.

Many critics gave *White Man, Listen!* good reviews. Even a few newspapers in the South were receptive to it. Other reviewers, however, attacked Wright's writing style as well as his views about white oppression. After so many years without a best-selling book, Wright focused on the negative reviews and questioned his future as a writer.

The novel Wright was working on was *The Long Dream*. The story concerned a father and son, Tyree and Fishbelly Tucker, black middle-class residents of a Mississippi town. Tyree, the

Wright appears with a copy of his book White Man, Listen! *which was published in 1957.*

father, is an "Uncle Tom," a subservient Southern black man who tries not to do anything to upset the whites in town. Despite his attitude, Tyree ends up murdered by the town's white chief of police. Tyree's son, Fishbelly, at first follows in his father's footsteps, but then is framed for a crime he did not commit. Rather than try to work within the corrupt system of politics and racism, Fishbelly decides to leave the country and move to Paris.

Wright wrote much of *The Long Dream* at Ailly in the first half of 1957. He sent it off to Aswell in New York. Aswell liked the book well enough to accept it. Wright then began outlining a sequel, about Fishbelly Tucker in Paris.

But Wright's heart was not fully in his work. He felt physically exhausted, perhaps because of his extensive travels, perhaps as a result of his hard work on *The Long Dream*. His fatigue was compounded by emotional strain. From Jackson, Mississippi, came the news that Wright's aunt Maggie had died. Aunt Maggie was his mother's caretaker, so Wright not only suffered the grief of this loss, but also concern about his mother. She decided to move back to Chicago to live with Wright's brother, Leon.

Wright no longer felt comfortable living in France. The country was engaged in a bloody war with its North African colony, Algeria, whose people were fighting for independence. The racial tolerance Wright had always appreciated about France now became strained.

Wright spent much of his time writing in 1957, completing the novel The Long Dream.

He saw racial discrimination against dark-skinned Algerians. In addition, Wright felt a strain in the black American expatriate community in Paris. Over the years, he had made some enemies of other writers. And some U.S. citizens living abroad traded rumors about fellow Americans who were supposedly working as spies. While some people whispered that Wright was an FBI informant, Wright worried that the U.S. government was stirring up trouble for him. He and Ellen talked of moving to London.

"COME BACK!"

But Wright stayed in France. He found peace and enjoyment at his farm in Ailly. While there in the summer of 1958, he wrote

Wright exits the farmhouse at Ailly. The farm provided him a place to rest while dealing with the disappointing reviews for The Long Dream.

the sequel to *The Long Dream*, which he called *Island of Hallucinations*. But the end of the year brought more strain and sorrow. Doubleday published *The Long Dream* in October, and the critics were not impressed. They found Wright's portrait of the South and the characters and plot unrealistic. They again charged that Wright had lost touch with his native country.

African American writer and critic Nick Aaron Ford called the novel "a colossal disappointment." He noted, "Wright is fighting a battle that has already been conceded. . . . The battle has moved up to a higher realm. The targets now are equality of job opportunity, the right to vote in the deep South, integrated housing, and integrated schools."

African American scholar Saunders Redding wrote in the *New York Times Book Review*, "'The Long Dream' proves that Wright has been away too long. . . . Come back, Dick Wright, to life again!"

But Wright did not even consider going back to the United States. His wife had developed a busy career as a literary agent. His older daughter, Julia, planned to go to Cambridge University in London. Rachel, his younger daughter, was a native French speaker. And Wright still feared that his two girls would face racial hatred if they lived in the United States.

More bad news followed the bad reviews. From Chicago, Wright's brother telegraphed that their mother was very sick. Leon and Ella needed money. Wright had enjoyed financial security for years from *Black Boy* and *Native Son*, but the income from those books had run its course. Wright worried about money. He had to borrow money from his agent, Paul Reynolds, to send to Leon.

Then, in November 1958, Wright's editor, Edward Aswell, died unexpectedly. Wright deeply felt the loss of this man who had supported his career so steadily. Two months later Ella Wright died. Wright and his mother had inhabited different worlds, but he felt deep sorrow. Ella had taught the famous writer how to read.

SETBACKS AND SICKNESS

Paul Reynolds read the manuscript for *Island of Hallucinations* and did not think it could be published. In the novel, Fishbelly Tucker has flown to Paris, only to find the American expatriate community there in turmoil, with spies and rumors and back-biting. Wright's new editor at Doubleday did not like it any better. Lacking encouragement and inspiration, Wright set the novel aside.

In the spring of 1959, Wright had plans to travel to Africa again. He tried to obtain funding for the tour, but none of the cultural organizations he approached would back him.

Wright, in 1959

With sales of *The Long Dream* poor, and no major publication on the horizon, Wright faced serious financial difficulties. He and Ellen decided to leave Paris for London, where her career could flourish. To finance the move, Wright had to sell his beloved Ailly farm and give up the spacious apartment on rue Monsieur le Prince. Ellen and the girls moved to London in the summer of 1959, while Wright rented a two-room apartment in a quiet Paris neighborhood. British immigration officials had balked at granting him an immigration visa. Still, he assumed that he would be able to immigrate to Great Britain and join his family in London in a few months.

Then, at the end of June 1959, Wright became very sick with dysentery, an intestinal disease that causes severe diarrhea. Doctors speculated that he had contracted the disease during his travels in Africa. The illness came on suddenly and forcefully. He was exhausted, suffered abdominal pain, and ran frequent fevers.

Even while sick, Wright explored new creative opportunities. A South African writer introduced him to Japanese haiku poetry, and he became fascinated by it. He put together a new collection of short stories, which World Publishers agreed to publish under the title *Eight Men*. He toyed with the idea of starting a magazine that would explore the psychological and social underpinnings of murder and other serious crimes. The project did not materialize.

By the fall of 1959, Wright had recovered enough to visit his family in London. British immigration officials harassed him when he entered the country, and he realized that his request to immigrate permanently might not be granted. Shortly after Wright returned to Paris, he had to make another trip to Great Britain for the funeral of his old friend George Padmore, who had helped lead the Gold Coast to independence. The death of yet another influential person in his life deeply upset Wright.

To make matters worse, he encountered more resistance from British immigration officials when he met with them to discuss his immigration request. Although the officials did not flatly deny his request, Wright concluded that the government did not want him in Great Britain. He blamed it on racism and the government's desire to keep voices of dissent out of the country. Wright stopped pursuing his immigration visa. He would live in Paris, separate from his family.

PILES OF POETRY

Wright lived alone in Paris, but he was not completely on his own. He cooked for himself but employed a maid to clean and do his dishes. He saw good friends. To earn money, he wrote liner notes—essays included in record albums—as well as articles. Wright felt hopeful about a stage version of *The Long Dream*, written by Pulitzer Prize-winning playwright Ketti Frings, set to open in early 1960. When the play opened on Broadway on February 17, 1960, however, reviews were so poor that Frings decided to close down the production after only five shows.

After this failure, Wright was unhappy and unwell. His intestinal distress continued, often leaving him feverish and exhausted. He found a new doctor, who prescribed a bland diet and daily doses of bismuth, a pinkish-white metal used in medicines for upset stomachs. The doctor admired Wright's work and treated him without charge. Wright followed his doctor's prescriptions faithfully, but he could not gain back his strength.

In his weakened condition, Wright seemed to find solace in writing haiku. The poems each have only three lines and seventeen syllables. He carried a notebook full of haiku wherever he went. He counted syllables on napkins while seated in Paris cafés. He wrote as he lay in bed. He produced more than four thousand haiku by the spring of 1960.

Similar to the way he used to spread sections of his *Native Son* manuscript around his room, Wright fanned his haiku around

```
        I give permission
   For this slow spring rain to soak
        The violet beds.
```

```
    Make up your mind, Snail!
  You are half inside your house,
       And halfway out!
```

Wright wrote thousands of haiku, including the two shown here, which he typed up and hung around his office as a means of organizing them.

him so he could organize the poems into a possible book. His daughter Julia, who was eighteen years old, went to Paris to spend time with him. She later wrote, "I remember how he would hang pages and pages of [haiku] up, as if to dry, on long metal rods strung across the narrow office area of his tiny sunless studio in Paris, like the abstract still-life photographs he used to compose and develop himself at the beginning of his Paris exile. I also recall how one day he tried to teach me how to count the syllables: 'Julia, you can write them, too. It's always, five, and seven and five—like math. So you can't go wrong.'"

Wright's haiku reflected his own life and the natural world around him. They sometimes revealed his wit, which was known to his friends and acquaintances but rarely seen in his novels:

> O finicky cat,
> Forgive me for this spring rain
> That disgusts you so!

By the summer of 1960, Wright had selected 811 haiku and sent them off to an editor and friend at World Publishers. Much to Wright's disappointment, the company did not want to publish them.

ENDING ALONE

Wright pulled himself out of a period of depression to work again on *Island of Hallucinations* and to start a new short story. He still planned to return to Africa for a visit. And he was cheered by Julia's decision to leave Cambridge University to attend the Sorbonne University in Paris. She arrived in September 1960.

On November 8, Wright delivered a lecture at the American Church in Paris. In his speech, he presented an angry and depressing survey of black artists. Using examples from his own life and the lives of other black writers, he described a white-controlled world of publishing and arts that caused black artists to turn against each other, competing for the few slots available to blacks. He described a world in which U.S. agents spied on everyone. He even suggested that the U.S. government sponsored Communism and other revolutionary movements so that it could keep control of dissenters.

It was a strong and somewhat strange speech, but Wright was proud of it. He hoped to revise it and turn it into something he could publish. But Wright soon became sick with fever, dizziness, and intestinal problems. Friends and Julia cared for him at his small apartment. Although Wright felt a little better, he checked into a Paris clinic for tests on November 26.

By November 28, he was feeling stronger. Extensive medical tests had uncovered no explanation for his illness. He spoke by telephone with Ellen, who was in London. He reassured her with the news that he seemed to be better. He put in a call to his friend Oliver Harrington, who was not at home. Wright then sent him a telegram: "Ollie please come to see me as soon as you get this." Wright was scheduled to go home the next day.

About eleven o'clock that night, Wright died, alone in his room in the clinic. He had had a fatal heart attack at age fifty-two.

Epilogue: I Deal in Meaning

IN HIS INTRODUCTION TO *WHITE MAN, LISTEN!* Wright wrote, "Recently a young woman asked me: 'But would your ideas make people happy?' And, before I was aware of what I was saying, I heard myself answering with a degree of frankness that I rarely, in deference to politeness, permit myself in personal conversation: 'My dear, I do not deal in happiness; I deal in meaning.'"

Wright's death eluded the clear meaning that, as a writer, he might have liked to give it. Its suddenness struck some as suspicious. Oliver Harrington wondered why his friend sent him an urgent message just hours before he died—perhaps Wright feared someone was trying to kill him. Wright had mentioned this in his later years, as his suspicions about his enemies grew more intense. Other friends, as well as his daughter Julia, also thought he might have been targeted by government agents. "I was the only member of the Wright family present in Paris at the time of my father's death," Julia Wright wrote in 2007, "and one of the last persons to have seen him." She suspected that her father did not die of natural causes. But Ellen Wright believed that her husband finally succumbed to dysentery, complicated by the stresses of his later life. Wright's leading biographers eventually came to share this view. Although Wright spoke out against racism in the United States and elsewhere, he did not seem to be of such concern to any government as to be a target for assassination.

Wright's family and a few close friends attended a ceremony at which his body was cremated on December 3, 1960. The precise cause of his death remains unknown. His ashes are buried at Père Lachaise in Paris, a cemetery with the graves of many prominent people who lived in France.

Wright's ashes were buried within this building at the Père Lachaise cemetery. Many people visit this cemetery every year to see the graves of the famous people buried there.

Wright's life did "deal in meaning." The writer Irving Howe aptly suggested the meaning of Wright's struggle:

> He told us the one thing even the most liberal and well-disposed whites preferred not to hear: that Negroes were far from patient or forgiving, that they were scarred by fear, that they hated every moment of their humiliation even when seeming most acquiescent, and that often enough they hated us, the decent and cultivated white men who, from complicity or neglect, shared in the responsibility for their plight.

Richard Wright told white Americans and the world that the United States was deforming the lives and spirits of black people. He spread his message through violent, difficult books that attracted more readers than any other black writer before him. As a successful writer, he encouraged and influenced other African American writers, including Margaret Walker, Ralph Ellison, Gwendolyn Brooks, and James Baldwin. Yet he enjoyed remarkably little encouragement and made his way mostly on his own—alone. Perhaps this is how it had to be. He did not complain about it. To the contrary, he wrote:

> I declare unabashedly that I like and even cherish the state of abandonment, of aloneness; it does not bother me; indeed, to me it seems the natural, inevitable condition of man, and I welcome it.
> —*White Man, Listen!*

Chronology of Richard Wright's Life

1908	Richard Nathaniel Wright is born to Ella and Nathan Wright, September 4, Adams County, Mississippi.
1910	Leon Wright, Richard's brother, is born.
1911	The Wright family moves in with Ella's parents, Richard and Margaret Wilson, in Natchez, Mississippi.
1913	The Wrights leave the Wilsons and move to Memphis, Tennessee.
1914	Nathan Wright leaves his family, although he still lives in Memphis.
1916	Ella Wright falls ill and places Richard and Leon in an orphanage. In the summer, Ella and the two boys move in with her parents again, in Jackson, Mississippi. Later, Ella, Richard, and Leon move to Elaine, Arkansas. There they live with Ella's sister Maggie and her husband, Silas Hoskins.
1917	After Silas Hoskins is murdered, Ella and her sons move to West Helena, Arkansas.
1919	After Ella gets sick again, Richard and Ella go to live with Ella's parents in Jackson, Mississippi. Leon goes to Detroit, Michigan, to live with Ella's sister Maggie.

1921	Richard enrolls in the Jim Hill Public School.
1923	Richard enters the Smith Robertson School as an eighth-grader.
1925	Richard graduates from Smith Robertson School. Determined to earn enough money to make his way north, he gets various jobs after graduation. By year's end, he moves to Memphis, Tennessee.
1926	Richard works at an optical company in Memphis.
1927	Richard pays for his mother and Leon to join him in Memphis. Maggie, Ella's sister, joins them. Richard and Maggie move to Chicago.
1928	In Chicago, Wright lives in the black ghetto of the city's South Side. He is hired as a temporary employee at the post office. His savings enable him to pay for Ella and Leon to move to Chicago.
1929	After a crash weight-gain diet, Wright achieves the minimum weight for permanent post office employment and gets a permanent post office job.
1930	As a result of the Great Depression, Wright loses his post office job.
1933	Wright attends his first meeting of the Communist-affiliated John Reed Club in Chicago. He begins writing poetry with revolutionary themes.
1934	Left-wing journals publish Wright's poems, and Wright joins the Communist Party. He gets a government-sponsored job at the South Side Boys' Club.
1935	Wright visits New York City, as a delegate to the Communist Party's American Writers' Congress. Returning to Chicago, He starts a new job with the Federal Writers' Project.

1936	Wright's short story, "Big Boy Leaves Home," is published in an anthology and receives warm praise.
1937	Wright moves to New York City, where he works for the Communist newspaper, the *Daily Worker.* He submits short stories to a contest held by *Story* magaz ine and learns in December that he is the winner.
1938	Harper & Brothers accepts the stories Wright submitted to the *Story* contest for publication as a book, entitled *Uncle Tom's Children.* Harper & Brothers gives him a contract to write a new novel.
1939	Wright is awarded a Guggenheim Fellowship. He devotes himself to writing full-time. He finishes his novel for Harper & Brothers, which he calls *Native Son.* In August, he marries Dhimah Meadman.
1940	*Native Son* is published. A selection of the Book-of-the-Month Club, the novel becomes a best seller.
1941	Divorced from Dhimah, Wright marries Ellen Poplar. A stage version of *Native Son* opens on Broadway. Wright's *12 Million Black Voices* is published. He quits the Communist Party.
1942	The Wrights become parents with the birth of their daughter, Julia.
1943	Wright works on his autobiography, which he calls *American Hunger.* He later changes the title to *Black Boy.*
1945	*Black Boy* is published in March and is a best seller.
1947	Wright and his wife and daughter move to Paris.
1949	The Wrights' second daughter, Rachel, is born. Wright works on a screenplay for a film version of *Native Son* and travels to the United States and Argentina for months of filming.

1951	*Native Son*, the movie, is released.
1953	*The Outsider*, Wright's new novel, is published. Wright travels to the Gold Coast in Africa, to research a nonfiction book.
1954	Wright's book on his visit to the Gold Coast, called *Black Power*, is published. Wright travels to Spain to research a nonfiction book.
1955	Wright travels to Bandung, Indonesia, to observe a conference of the independent nations of Asia and Africa.
1956	*The Color Curtain*, Wright's book on the Bandung conference, is published.
1957	*Pagan Spain*, Wright's book on Spain, is published. Later in the year, a collection of his lectures, *White Man, Listen!* is published.
1958	Wright's new novel, *The Long Dream*, is published.
1959	Ellen Wright moves to London with Julia and Rachel. Wright expects to follow but cannot get permission from British officials to immigrate into Great Britain. He becomes ill with dysentery. He begins writing haiku and also compiles a new short-story collection, entitled *Eight Men*.
1960	Wright dies at the age of 52.
1961	Wright's short-story collection, *Eight Men*, is published.
1963	A previously unpublished novel, *Lawd Today*, is published.
1977	A complete version of Wright's autobiography, including a large section that was cut from *Black Boy*, is published as *American Hunger*.
1994	*Rite of Passage* is published.
1998	Wright's haiku collection is published as *Haiku: This Other World*.

Source Notes

9 Quoted in Hazel Rowley, *Richard Wright: The Life and Times* (New York: Henry Holt, 2001), 349.

13 Richard Wright, *Black Boy (American Hunger)* (New York: HarperPerennial, 1993), 8.

13 Ibid.

15 Ibid., 19.

16 Ibid., 21.

16 Ibid., 26.

19 Ibid., 45–46.

20 Ibid., 39.

20 Ibid., 40.

22 Ibid., 50.

25 Ibid., 103.

28 Ibid., 126.

28 Peter Lennon, "One of Uncle Tom's Children," *The Guardian*, December 8, 1960, in Keneth Kinnamon and Michel Fabre, eds., *Conversations with Richard Wright* (Jackson: University Press of Mississippi, 1993), 240.

28 Wright, *Black Boy*, 137.

29 Ibid., 147.

31 Ibid., 168.

31 Ibid., 172.

35 Ibid., 229.

37 Ibid., 246.

38 Ibid., 248.

38 Marcia Minor, "An Author Discusses His Craft," *Daily Worker*, December 13, 1938, in Kinnamon and Fabre, *Conversations with Richard Wright*, 16.

41 Georges Charbonnier, "The American Novel," October 1960, in Kinnamon and Fabre, *Conversations with Richard Wright*, 215.

45 Wright, *Black Boy*, 299.

52 Ibid., 318.

55 Ibid., 331.

59 Richard Wright, "Between the World and Me," in Ellen Wright and Michel Fabre, eds., *Richard Wright Reader* (New York: Da Capo Press, 1997), 247.

61 Roy Wilder, "Wright, Negro Ex-Field Hand, Looks Ahead to New Triumphs," *New York Herald Tribune*, August 17, 1941, in Kinnamon and Fabre, *Conversations with Richard Wright*, 39.

61 Margaret Walker Alexander, "Richard Wright," in Richard Macksey and Frank Moorer, *Richard Wright: A Collection of Essays* (Englewood Cliffs, N.J.: Prentice-Hall, 1984), 28.

63 Richard Wright, "Between Laughter and Tears," *New Masses* (October 5, 1937), in Stephen Railton, "Zora Neale Hurston Home Page," *American Literature Since 1865*, University of Virginia, N.d., http://etext.virginia.edu/railton/enam312/znhhp.html (April 10, 2007).

63 Richard Wright, "Blueprint for Negro Writing," in Wright and Fabre, *Richard Wright Reader*, 37.

64 Rowley, *Richard Wright: The Life and Times*, 131.

67 Quoted in Michel Fabre, *The Unfinished Quest of Richard Wright*, 2nd ed. (Urbana: University of Illinois Press, 1993), 162.

67 Zora Neale Hurston, "Stories of Conflict," in Henry Louis Gates Jr. and K. A. Appiah, eds., *Richard Wright: Critical Perspectives Past and Present* (New York: Amistad Press, 1993), 3.

68 Richard Wright, "How 'Bigger' Was Born," in *Native Son* (New York: HarperPerennial, 1998), 454.

68 Ibid., 457.

70 Alexander, "Richard Wright," in Macksey and Moorer, *Richard Wright: A Collection of Essays*, 32.

72 Wright, *Native Son*, 19–20.

73 Ibid., 429.

75 Clifton Fadiman, [Untitled Review of *Native Son*], in Gates and Appiah, *Critical Perspectives*, 6.

77 "Negro Hailed As New Writer," *New York Sun*, March 4, 1940, in Kinnamon and Fabre, *Conversations with Richard Wright*, 28.

77 Quoted in Fabre, *The Unfinished Quest of Richard Wright*, 202.

84 Ibid., 217.

86 Richard Wright, *12 Million Black Voices* (New York: Thunder's Mouth Press, 1988), 10.

86 Ibid., 12.

86 Matthew M. Briones, "Call-and-Response: Tracing the Ideological Shifts of Richard Wright through His Correspondence with Friends and Fellow Literati," *African American Review*, Spring 2003, 53.

91 Quoted in Fabre, *The Unfinished Quest of Richard Wright*, 249.

92 Quoted in "How Richard Wright Looks at *Black Boy*," *PM*, April 15, 1945, in Kinnamon and Fabre, *Conversations with Richard Wright*, 64–65.

93 "Richard Wright Papers, Image ID 1029030," Yale Collection of American Literature, Beinecke Rare Book & Manuscript Library, 1994, http://webtext.library.yale.edu/xml2html/beinecke.WRIGHT.con.html (April 10, 2007).

93 "Richard Wright Papers, Image ID 1029060-62," Yale Collection of American Literature, Beinecke Rare Book & Manuscript Library, 1994, http://webtext.library.yale.edu/xml2html/beinecke.WRIGHT.con.html (April 10, 2007).

93 Richard Wright, *Later Works: Black Boy (American Hunger)/The Outsider* (New York: Library of America, 1991), 869.

94 "Office Memorandum to Director, FBI, from SAC, New York City, February 26, 1945," in "Richard Nathaniel Wright," *Federal Bureau of Investigation, Freedom of Information Act*, N.d., http://foia.fbi.gov/foiaindex/rnwright.htm (April 10, 2007).

94 Ibid.

95 Quoted in Rowley, *Richard Wright: The Life and Times*, 306–7.

96 Wright, *Black Boy*, 37.

97 Quoted in "How Richard Wright Looks at *Black Boy*," 65.

102 Quoted in Rowley, *Richard Wright: The Life and Times*, 330.

103 Maurice Nadeau, "There's No Black Problem in the U.S.A., but a White Problem, the Black Writer Richard Wright Tells Us," *Combat*, May 11, 1946, in Kinnamon and Fabre, *Conversations with Richard Wright*, 88.

103 Ibid.

103 Anne Perlman, "Richard Wright, Negro Author, Is Here to Make Home in Paris," *New York Herald Tribune* (Paris edition), June 3, 1946, in Kinnamon and Fabre, *Conversations with Richard Wright*, 91.

105 Lucienne Escoube, "No Film Has Ever Depicted the Life of Blacks in American Cities," *L'Ecran français*, November 19, 1946, in Kinnamon and Fabre, *Conversations with Richard Wright*, 114.

105 "Why Richard Wright Came Back from France," *Sunday Picture News*, February 16, 1947, in Kinnamon and Fabre, *Conversations with Richard Wright*, 122.

106 Ibid., 123.

106 Ibid., 125.

109 Oliver W. Harrington, *Why I Left America and Other Essays* (Jackson: University Press of Mississippi, 1993), 8.

114 Quoted in Fabre, *The Unfinished Quest of Richard Wright*, 370.

114 Steven Marcus, "The American Negro in Search of History," in Gates and Appiah, *Richard Wright: Critical Perspectives Past and Present*, 35–36.

120 Richard Wright, *Pagan Spain* (New York: HarperPerennial, 1995), 4.

125 Harrington, *Why I Left America and Other Essays*, 9.

125 Quoted in Fabre, *The Unfinished Quest of Richard Wright*, 431.

127 Quoted in Addison Gayle, *Richard Wright: Ordeal of a Native Son* (New York: Anchor Press/Doubleday, 1980), 262.

129 Roi Ottley, "He Should Stick to Fiction," in Gates and Appiah, *Richard Wright: Critical Perspectives Past and Present*, 56.

133 Nick Aaron Ford, "A Long Way from Home," in Gates and Appiah, *Richard Wright: Critical Perspectives Past and Present*, 60.

133. Saunders Redding, "The Way It Was," in Gates and Appiah, *Richard Wright: Critical Perspectives Past and Present*, 60–61.

137 Richard Wright, *Haiku: This Other World* (New York: Arcade Publishing, 1998), viii.

138 Ibid., 2.

139 Quoted in *Richard Wright: Ordeal of a Native Son*, 299.

140 Richard Wright, *White Man, Listen! Lectures in Europe, 1950–1956* (New York: HarperPerennial, 1995), xxix.

141 Julia Wright, Personal correspondence with the author, January 23, 2007.

142 Irving Howe, "Richard Wright: A Word of Farewell," in Gates and Appiah, *Richard Wright: Critical Perspectives Past and Present*, 62.

142 Wright, *White Man, Listen!*, xxix.

Selected Bibliography

Bloom, Harold, ed. *Richard Wright: Modern Critical Views*. New York: Chelsea House, 1987.

Campbell, James. "Black American in Paris." *The Nation*, September 27, 2004. www.thenation.com/doc/20040927/campbell

———. *Exiled in Paris*. New York: Scribner, 1995.

Fabre, Michel. *The Unfinished Quest of Richard Wright*, 2nd ed. Urbana: University of Illinois Press, 1993.

Felgar, Robert. *Richard Wright*. Boston: Twayne Publishers, 1980.

Gates, Henry Louis, Jr., and K. A. Appiah, eds. *Richard Wright: Critical Perspectives Past and Present*. New York: Amistad Press, 1993.

Gayle, Addison. *Richard Wright: Ordeal of a Native Son*. New York: Anchor Press/Doubleday, 1980.

Harrington, Oliver W. *Why I Left America and Other Essays*. Jackson: University Press of Mississippi, 1993.

Kinnamon, Keneth, and Michel Fabre, eds. *Conversations with Richard Wright*. Jackson: University Press of Mississippi, 1993.

Macksey, Richard, and Frank E. Moorer, eds. *Richard Wright: A Collection of Essays*. Englewood Cliffs, N.J.: Prentice-Hall, Inc., 1984.

Native Son [videorecording]. International Film Forum, 1988.

"Richard Nathaniel Wright." *Federal Bureau of Investigation, Freedom of Information Act*, N.d. http://foia.fbi.gov/foiaindex/wright.htm.

"Richard Wright, Black Boy: A Moving Look at the Influential and Famous Writer Who Changed the Face of American Literature." *Independent Television Service (ITVS)*, N.d. www.itvs.org/RichardWright/index.html.

"The Richard Wright Connection." *C.L.R. James Institute*, January 17, 2003. www.clrjamesinstitute.org/index.html.

Richard Wright Papers. Yale Collection of American Literature, Beinecke Rare Book and Manuscript Library, 2006. http://library.yale.edu/beinecke.

Rowley, Hazel. *Richard Wright: The Life and Times*. New York: Henry Holt and Company, 2001.

———. "A Sort of Homecoming." *The Nation*, September 11, 2006. www.thenation.com/doc/20060911/rowley

Walker, Margaret. *Richard Wright, Daemonic Genius*. New York: Warner Books, 1988.

Wright, Ellen, and Michel Fabre, eds. *Richard Wright Reader*. New York: Da Capo Press, 1997.

Further Reading and Websites

BOOKS

Aberjhani, and Sandra L. West, eds. *Encyclopedia of the Harlem Renaissance.* New York: Facts On File, 2003.

Andrews, William L., Frances Smith Foster, and Trudier Harris, eds. *The Oxford Companion to African American Literature.* New York: Oxford University Press, 1997.

Damon, Duane. *Headin' for Better Times.* Minneapolis: Twenty-First Century Books, 2002.

Finlayson, Reggie. *We Shall Overcome.* Minneapolis: Twenty-First Century Books, 2003

Gates, Henry Louis, Jr., and Cornel West. *The African-American Century: How Black Americans Have Shaped Our Country.* New York: The Free Press, 2000.

Gottfried, Ted. *The Road to Communism.* Minneapolis: Twenty-First Century Books, 2002.

Hudson, Wade, ed. *Powerful Words: More Than 200 Years of Extraordinary Writing by African Americans.* New York: Scholastic, 2004.

Huggins, Nathan Irvin, ed. *Voices from the Harlem Renaissance.* New York: Oxford University Press, 1995.

Mitchell, Hayley R., ed. *Readings on Native Son.* San Diego: Greenhaven Press, 2000.

Sherman, Josepha. *The Cold War.* Minneapolis: Twenty-First Century Books, 2004.

WEBSITES

"American Life Histories: Manuscripts from the Federal Writers' Project." *Library of Congress.*
http://lcweb2.loc.gov/ammem/wpaintro/wpahome.html
This site reproduces work by writers who worked for the Federal Writers' Project (FWP) in the 1930s. In a section called "Voice from the Thirties," the website provides an introduction to the FWP and includes striking photographs.

"Chicago Renaissance: 1932–1950." *Chicago Public Library Online.*
http://www.chipublib.org/digital/chiren/introduc tion.html
This overview of the lively arts and culture scene that developed among African Americans in Chicago during the time Wright lived there is enhanced by illustrations from the Chicago Public Library's research collection. Clear and well-written, this is an excellent introduction to the environment that helped shape Wright.

Jim Crow Museum. Ferris State University.
www.ferris.edu/news/jimcrow/menu.htm
The website of the Jim Crow Museum in Big Rapids, Michigan, includes essays on topics relating to racism and discrimination, including extensive information on the Jim Crow system of legalized race discrimination that existed in the American South during Richard Wright's life.

Reading Wright Himself

Uncle Tom's Children: Four Novellas. 1938.

Native Son. 1940.

12 Million Black Voices: A Folk History of the Negro in the United States. 1941.

Black Boy: A Record of Childhood and Youth. 1945.

The Outsider. 1953.

Black Power: A Record of Reactions in a Land of Pathos. 1954.

Savage Holiday. 1954.

The Color Curtain: A Report on the Bandung Conference. 1956.

Pagan Spain: A Report of a Journey into the Past. 1956.

White Man, Listen! 1957.

The Long Dream. 1958.

POSTHUMOUS PUBLICATIONS

Eight Men. 1961.

Lawd Today. 1963.

American Hunger. 1977.

Rite of Passage. 1994.

Haiku: This Other World. 1998.

Index

About the Author

Debbie Levy is the author of many children's books on subjects ranging from bigotry to sunken treasure to U.S. presidents to the Vietnam War. Her books also include fiction and poetry. Before she started writing books for children, Debbie practiced law with a large Washington, D.C., law firm and worked as a newspaper editor. She has a bachelor's degree in government and foreign affairs from the University of Virginia, as well as a law degree and master's degree in world politics from the University of Michigan. Debbie enjoys paddling around in kayaks and canoes and fishing in the Chesapeake Bay region. She and her family live in Maryland.

Photo Acknowledgments

The images in the book are used with the permission of: Library of Congress, pp. 2 (LC-USW3-030278-D), 12 (LC-USZ62-125825), 20 (LC-USZ62-133436), 35 (LC-USZ62-130357), 36 (LC-USZ62-18532-31266), 38 (LC-USZC2-5810), 48, 66 (LC-USZ62-111624), 69 (LC-USZ62-112302), 102 (LC-USZ62-103679), 127 (LC-DIG-ppmsca-08092); From the Richard Wright Papers, Yale Collection of American Literature, Beinecke Rare Book and Manuscript Library, pp. 15, 25, 42, 54, 71, 74, 76, 80, 83, 84, 92, 104, 106, 111, 112, 113, 115, 117, 130, 132, (Courtesy of Michel Fabre, pp. 8, 32, 79, 134), (Copyright © 1953/1957 Richard Wright, Reprinted by permission of John Hawkins & Associates, Inc., pp. 118, 121, 122, 124); © Ed Clark/Time Life Pictures/Getty Images, pp. 16, 19; Mississippi Department of Archives and History, pp. 27, 30; National Archives, pp. 43, 58; © Culver Pictures, pp. 49, 60, 84 (inset); © Getty Images, pp. 50, 51, 131; General Research Division, The New York Public Library, Astor, Lenox and Tilden Foundations, p. 53; General Research & Reference Division, Schomburg Center for Research in Black Culture, The New York Public Library, Astor, Lenox and Tilden Foundations, p. 63; © Ben Martin/Time Life Pictures/Getty Images, p. 64; Reprinted with permission of *The News & Observer* of Raleigh, North Carolina, Courtesy of the North Carolina State Archives, p. 82; © Bettmann/CORBIS, p. 89; Book cover from BLACK BOY by RICHARD WRIGHT Copyright 1937, 1942, 1944, 1945 by Richard Wright; renewed © 1973 by Ellen Wright. Reprinted by permission of HarperCollins Publishers. Image courtesy of Richard Wright Papers, Yale Collection of American Literature, Beinecke Rare Book and Manuscript Library, p. 96; Milstein Division of United States History, Local History & Genealogy, The New York Public Library, Astor, Lenox and Tilden Foundations, p. 99; Nelson Algren Papers, The Rare Books and Manuscripts Library of The Ohio State University Libraries, p. 108; Copyright © 1998 by Ellen Wright, Reprinted from *Haiku: This Other World* by Richard Wright, published by Arcade Publishing, New York, New York. Image courtesy of Richard Wright Papers, Yale Collection of American Literature, Beinecke Rare Book and Manuscript Library, p. 137; © Robert Holmes/CORBIS, p. 141.

Front Cover: © Culver Pictures